MANAGING STUDENT ASSISTANTS

A How-To-Do-It Manual for Librarians®

KIMBERLY BURKE SWEETMAN

HOW TO DO IT MANUALS
FOR LIBRARIANS

NUMBER 155

NEAL-SCHUMAN PUBLISHERS, INC.
New York   London

Published by Neal-Schuman Publishers, Inc.
100 William St., Suite 2004
New York, NY 10038

Printed and bound in the United States of America.

The paper used in this publication meets the minimum requirements of American National Standard for Information Sciences—Permanence of Paper for Printed Library Materials, ANSI Z39.48-1992.

ISBN-13: 978-1-55570-581-7
ISBN-10: 1-55570-581-2

Library of Congress Cataloging-in-Publication Data

Sweetman, Kimberly Burke.
   Managing student assistants : a how-to-do-it manual for librarians / Kimberly Burke Sweetman.
        p. cm. — (How to do it manuals for librarians ; no. 155)
   Includes bibliographical references and index.
   ISBN 1-55570-581-2 (alk. paper)
  1. Student library assistants. 2. Library personnel management. 3. Academic libraries—Personnel management. I. Title. II. Series: How-to-do-it manuals for libraries ; no. 155.
   Z682.4.S89S94 2007
   023'.3—dc22
                                                                    2006014896

To Peter

For his continued love and support through the process and beyond

CONTENTS

LIST OF FIGURES

PREFACE

The majority of academic and research libraries could not function without a large contingent of student assistants. They are a workforce capable of performing a range of tasks—as routine as labeling and shelving and as complex as processing archival material and assisting with interlibrary loans. Although students can execute a variety of jobs, they all require a special kind of attention. Novice librarians often receive supervisory responsibility over these workers, but few have experience managing them. Likewise, seasoned professionals often find the challenges posed by this group to be daunting. *Managing Student Assistants: A How-To-Do-It Manual for Librarians* offers practical advice for creative ways to recruit, train, and retain this essential part of the staff.

I had never focused on management in the process of getting my MLS degree. And yet, as part of my first appointment, I was given responsibility for a small cadre of student assistants. I also had the good fortune to be placed under the guidance of a skilled library manager. As I learned best practices for management from my supervisor, I put them into practice with my mini-staff. This combination helped me to slowly learn the fundamentals of library supervision. Since then, I have managed large academic library departments staffed by dozens of workers, both in the United States and abroad, always with some mix of students.

WHY BOTHER WITH STUDENT ASSISTANTS?

Too often I hear supervisors describe the process of building an effective team of student workers as unworthy of the effort. They complain that it is a waste of time to invest in temporary workers. Many librarians are of the attitude that such helpers are expendable: they don't spend any time training, orienting, or developing their part-time staff in any way, believing that student workers do not last long enough in the job to merit such an investment.

I disagree wholeheartedly. My experience, coupled with that of some of my colleagues, shows that if you invest the time in workers—selecting them carefully, training them thoroughly, and providing them with continual challenges—they give excellent work in return. They not only make lasting commitments to their part-time jobs, but a surprising percentage also go on to pursue careers in library work.

The primary goal of *Managing Student Assistants* is to encourage supervisors to see the value—and sometimes necessity—of taking seriously assistants drawn from their academic communities. This volume illustrates the steps involved in getting to that point, whether you are looking to improve or expand an existing program — or looking to hire your first helpers.

ORGANIZATION

Managing Student Assistants: A How-To-Do-It Manual for Librarians is organized into seven chapters. I begin with the basics then move through planning, recruiting, hiring, and retention strategies.

Chapter 1, "The Basics of Managing Student Assistants," builds the case for employing students at your library. It lays out the primary advantages of this workforce and offers suggestions for overcoming the perceived disadvantages. This chapter also offers guidance for adapting some basic supervisory skills to the needs of students.

Chapter 2, "Preparing to Recruit Student Assistants," helps to determine where students might fit into your organization. By performing an accurate workflow analysis, you will learn how best to design the job, request approval, and secure funding.

Chapter 3, "Simplifying the Hiring Process," looks at two essential elements of hiring student workers: an effective job description and a vacancy toolkit. The first part of this chapter helps you to draft a job description with attention paid to specifying required competencies. The second helps you to assemble a vacancy toolkit that brings together checklists, schedules, scripts, and worksheets to take you through the hiring process.

Chapter 4, "Recruiting and Responding to Candidates," offers ideas for advertising the position and replying effectively to applicants. As students have different interests from professionals, it is important to advertise professionally and time your announcement carefully. This is also the first opportunity to shape your applicant pool, thus responding appropriately to interested parties is important.

Chapter 5, "Interviewing and Selecting Candidates," guides you through preparation, execution, and follow-through for the interview. You will learn how to question candidates thoroughly, professionally, fairly, and legally. There are suggestions for checking references and guidance for selecting your final candidate.

Chapter 6, "Training and Orienting New Workers," provides several tools and suggestions for initiating your new employee. You will find an orientation checklist that helps you determine the necessary areas with which your new student assistant will need to be familiar and tips for delivering that orientation effectively. There is also coverage of special training issues, including customer service, policy enforcement, and even training for supervision of other students.

Chapter 7, "Keeping Performance High and Turnover Low," suggests strategies for maintaining performance and minimizing turnover. If students are to be an important part of your staff, you will want to increase their areas of responsibility and retain their services for as long as possible. In addition to retention strategies, you will also find advice for evaluating, coaching, and motivating students through their tenure at your institution.

Throughout the chapters, you will find numerous management exercises to build your skills and create a successful student employment program. I have included tips, typical manager questions and answers, and a reoccurring "Manager's Roundtable"—other managers from institutions with diverse locations and student populations—to weigh in on important issues. Additional sources at the end of the book include a bibliography, Web links to recommended policies and procedures, and a sample student worker handbook.

Managing Student Assistants: A How-To-Do-It Manual for Librarians outlines the key strategies for successfully recruiting and retaining high-quality workers that will increase your departmental productivity. Student workers can make an important contribution to the library when you invest the time to create an efficient program to manage their selection, training, and development. I hope you can turn this often underutilized group of employees into a vital part of your team.

ACKNOWLEDGMENTS

As with any major project, I did not complete this book on my own. Several people contributed to its completion, some of whom may not be aware of their role in its development. This book has its origins in a workshop I first developed in 2000. I owe a tremendous debt to Susan Salomone, then the professional development coordinator at the Metropolitan New York Library Council, who originally suggested that I develop a workshop on the topic and provided a tremendous amount of encouragement while I designed the workshop. I would also like to thank Tim Johnson and Dottie Heibing at the Metropolitan New York Library Council for allowing me to explore this and other management topics by designing workshops on them, and to thank the students of these classes for their great suggestions. Teaching workshops, ironically, has been a tremendous source of learning for me.

Thanks are also due to Miguel Figueroa and Michael Kelley at Neal-Schuman. Miguel initially suggested that I develop the topic into a book, and Michael shared his considerable talent by walking me through the process and providing encouragement and feedback.

Many thanks to Susan Lorenzo, my supervisor at my first professional job, who provided me not only with an opportunity to supervise student assistants, but more importantly provided me with a terrific supervisory role model. Thanks also to all of the student assistants whom I have supervised over the years, without whom this book would not have been possible.

I am grateful to all of my colleagues who provided anecdotes for inclusion in this volume, and to June Power and Matt Rohde who provided the perfect examples of training materials. I could not have asked for better examples for inclusion in this volume. A special thank-you to my panel of experts: Scott Hanscom, Werner Haun, Bonnie Hines, Conni Kitten, Michael Miller, Gary Ploski, and Nick Rizzo. A special thank-you to Cathy Von Elm, not only for reading an early draft but also for suggesting several members of the panel of experts.

Thanks to New York University for providing much needed research leave to complete this project and to Kristina Rose, who filled in so ably during my absence. Thanks to my friends and family for supporting me through the process, especially my "homework partner" Nadaleen Tempelman-Kluit, who shared countless hours of research and editing time with me while she completed her own project. Most of all, thanks to my wonderful husband, Peter, who provided me with the love and support I needed to complete this project.

1 THE BASICS OF MANAGING STUDENT ASSISTANTS

A BRIEF HISTORY OF EMPLOYING STUDENT ASSISTANTS

> There is nothing a well trained student couldn't do under careful supervision. Those who do not know how to organize and manage such help [are the ones who] so strenuously object to being bothered with student assistants.
> —Mary Elizabeth Downey, *Library Journal*, 1932

In his 1995 article, "The Evolving Role of Student Employees in Academic Libraries," David Gregory highlights the trends in hiring student library assistants throughout the twentieth century. Student assistants are mentioned in the professional literature as early as 1910, when Laura Gibbs describes them in the *ALA Bulletin* as "economical and satisfactory" for routine tasks like card filing and book repair. The idea that student workers were not suitable for work with the public prevailed through the 1920s (Gregory, 1995: 5), but the professional literature of the 1930s indicates a trend toward student assistants working at the circulation desk which came with the recognition that students' familiarity with their campus was an asset (Gregory, 1995: 7, 9). Familiarity with campus remains an asset of student library assistants today, and, interestingly, student patrons are more apt to approach a student worker at the desk than someone outside of their peer group. Throughout the 1940s, student workers were assigned more varied tasks, at least at the liberal arts colleges and at this point in history it was common for students to work at the circulation desk in all types of academic libraries. It is during the 1940s that the literature first mentions student library work as a learning experience for the employee (Gregory, 1995: 11) which seems in stark contrast to the prevailing notion quoted by Janice Burrows in her 1995 article, "Training Student Workers in Academic Libraries: How and Why." In the article she quotes Emile C. White, writing during the 1940s that student workers are relied upon to, "at the very least . . . constitute a labor reserve for the monotonous and repetitious tasks that are necessary for successful library operation" (Gregory, 1995:

Meet the Panel of Experts in Our Managers' Roundtable Discussion

Throughout the book, our colleagues offer expert opinions on managing student library assistants. These colleagues have years of supervisory experience and work in various departments and libraries in the United States and Canada.

Scott Hanscom, Coordinator for Monograph Acquisitions and Rapid Cataloging, Milton S. Eisenhower Library, Johns Hopkins University, Baltimore, Maryland

Werner Haun, Collections Conservator and Head of Collections Care Section, Library of Congress, Washington, DC

Dr. Bonnie Hines, Associate Librarian, Louisiana State University at Alexandria

Conni Kitten, Library Associate, Document Delivery, Texas Tech University Libraries

Michael Miller, MLS, MS, Coordinator of Access Services, Benjamin Rosenthal Library, Queens College—City University of New York

Gary Ploski, Academic Computing Support Coordinator, Sarah Lawrence College

Nick Rizzo, Circulation and Office Manager, Education Library, University of British Columbia

78). While the journal literature published on managing student workers declined from the mid-1940s until the 1970s, nine master's theses were published on the topic during that time (Gregory, 1995: 12).

Throughout the 1970s the professional literature records a trend in employing students to improve the cultural diversity of library staff as well as a true diversity in the work that student assistants were charged with (Gregory, 1995: 15). In 1970, the first published study on the capabilities of student reference staff, based on a program at the State University in Cortland, New York, suggested that upper-level students could provide competent reference assistance in undergraduate libraries under minimal supervision, given adequate training (p. 13). From 1970 to 1995, the year Gregory's article was published, the literature focused on the achievements and creative use of student workers rather than their limitations (p. 15). For example, during this time there was increased debate over employing student assistants at reference desks and for other higher level work.

In 1990, the Association of Research Libraries (ARL) published the results of a survey of its member libraries on the topic of student employment. Every major research library responding to the survey reported relying on student assistants to shelve materials, staff public service desks when full-time staff was not available, and provide clerical support. Seventy percent of research libraries reported relying on students to process books prior to shelving, sort mail, repair books, and prepare materials for binding, and 94 percent relied on students to keep service desks open. Ninety-eight percent of respondents reported that students performed necessary work when other staff was not available. Yet the executive summary of the report suggests that students were not fully utilized (ARL, *Student Employment Programs in ARL Libraries: SPEC Kit 168*). While the ARL survey did not inquire about the percentage of student staffing as compared with all staff at the library, the National Center for Education Statistics reported that in 1996, 29.3 percent of staff in all postsecondary degree granting institutions' libraries were part-time, temporary student assistants (U.S. Dept. of Education, NCES, 2991: B9). A 2005 ARL survey reports that Access Services departments employ, on average, 23.6 student assistants, which rivals the average number of regular staff these departments employ, 23.1, and 75 percent of respondents to this survey report that their student workforce has increased in the past ten years (Dawes et al., 2005). ARL annual statistics suggest that student staffing may be tapering off in large research libraries, perhaps in response to increased automation. For the years 1999–2003, the median annual volumes added to ARL collections increased 4 percent while support staff at ARL libraries decreased 5 percent and student assistants at ARL libraries decreased 9 percent. Interestingly, over the same time period student assistants have consistently represented one-third of the non-MLS holding library workforce (*Association of Research Libraries*, www.fisher.lib.virginia.edu/arl).

Although the use of student workers is widespread, many academic libraries certainly could use their student workforce more effectively. As the nature of library service changes, staff responsibilities at all levels are changing rapidly. Keeping student workers in mind while planning your own work, as well as the work of the full-time staff in your area, can help you make more appropriate time management and workflow choices. Examining the tasks that a department performs and determining which level of staff is most appropriate to perform the tasks will keep a department running efficiently and also help to keep morale up for staff at all levels.

REAL ADVANTAGES TO HIRING STUDENTS

While it is a given that libraries around the world rely on student workers, many library supervisors feel reluctant to hire students or are disappointed in their current student worker program, commonly remarking that it is "more trouble than it is worth." For those who may be resistant to becoming reliant on students, I point our that there are numerous advantages to hiring student workers in all types of libraries. First and foremost, most libraries could not fully staff the great variety of programs and services they offer without employing students. As Burrows (1995) points out, the obvious advantage to hiring student workers is economical: they are cheap to employ (p. 78). But, there are certainly other advantages. For example, working in the library adds to a student's academic experience, not only by adding valuable job skills to his or her résumé, but also by helping the student become more comfortable with the library as a valuable academic resource. Furthermore, an effective student worker program may also help to recruit talented individuals to all levels of full-time library work.

THEY WILL HELP YOU GET THE WORK DONE

Student assistants are employed in just about every academic library in North America. If you need a compelling argument to justify hiring student workers, consider that, first and foremost, the work needs to get done, whether it be checking in books, maintaining computers, or unpacking new acquisitions. Service demand increases continually. Budgets are tight, and new initiatives can be started more quickly and more flexibly if staffed by students—in many cases new initiatives can only be begun if they are staffed by student assistants. A recent ARL survey showed that 75 percent of Access Services departments in ARL libraries have increased their student workforce in the past ten years (Dawes et al., 2005), which seems to correlate with increased services and programs. According to *The Status of*

Don't be apologetic about asking students to be productive at work. Remember, you and the student should benefit from his or her employment.

Academic Libraries in the United States: Results from the 1996 Academic Library Survey with Historical Comparisons, a report from the National Center for Education Statistics by Maggie Cahalan, Wendy Mansfield, and Natalie Justh, student assistants make up 29 percent of total academic library staff. Certain tasks simply could not be accomplished without employing students. Is there any college or university library that keeps up with checkout, shelving, or photocopying demand with full-time staff alone?

THE JOB WILL ENRICH THEIR ACADEMIC EXPERIENCE

Several studies indicate that having an on-campus job increases a student's likelihood of graduation. In their 2005 article, Kerkvliet and Nowell found, after tracking students for a year at Oregon State University, that work study encourages student retention, while grants do not, and that while having an on-campus job does not seem to affect student retention, higher wages at on-campus jobs do seem to correlate to higher student retention rates. DesJardins, Ahlburg, and McCall (1999) determined that student financial aid granted in exchange for work, like college work study, is more likely to prevent drop-out and stop-out (taking time off from school) than grants. In their 2002 study of students at the University of Minnesota, Des-Jardins et al. found that work study is the only type of financial aid that correlates to higher graduation rates (p. 570). They cite several studies that, like their own 1999 work, document that financial aid contributes to student success by more than merely providing educational funds, suggesting that a feeling of belonging at one's campus workplace may help to integrate students into campus life as a whole (p. 561). They also suggest that regular on-campus employment (without a work study award) is a worthy factor for study in comparison with student retention and graduation rates (p. 572).

My student assistants are always so unreliable, I feel like throwing in the towel and never hiring another student! Help!

Before you give up you should take a look at your standards. Be sure to check the references of applicants, to be sure you are hiring trustworthy student assistants. Do your homework before you hire. Also, carefully explain your expectations and the consequences of not meeting those expectations. Remember, you set the tone for your department; if you raise the standards for hiring and work performance your student workers will be more reliable.

Recently, much has been written about the behavioral and demographic characteristics of the "Millennial Generation"—those individuals born after 1981 who have graduated high school since 2000. Generally speaking, these children of Baby Boomers favor active learning over passive book or lecture learning (Wilson and Folz, pp. 61–62). Since they learn by doing, college students today are inclined to secure some type of employment, and most regard their work experience as a vital part of their educational experience. Some libraries understand this concept well. For example, San Jose State University considers employing student workers as part of its academic responsibility, stating that, "the Library serves as a resource for students by providing employment opportunities. By employing student assistants, the Library is enhancing their academic and personal growth. In return, student assistant employees are improving library service by representing a link to the student body at large" (www.sjlibrary.org/gateways/academic/affirm.htm). Indeed, by employing student assistants we all have a tremendous opportunity to enhance their academic and personal growth.

THE POLICY MAY RECRUIT NEW LIBRARIANS

Another reason to maintain a robust student assistant program is the need to recruit well-qualified, intelligent people to careers in library work. In collaboration with the Association for Research Libraries, Stanley Wilder has explored the age demographics of librarians, and has observed that librarians as a population are aging (and presumably will be retiring) at a faster rate than other professions. Wilder's original study, *The Age Demographics of Academic Librarians: A Profession Apart* (1995), predicts that retirements will have an enormous impact on the population of librarians at least through 2015. His 2003 update to this study states that, "25% of the 2000 population is age 55 and older and 13% of the 2005 population is predicted to be 60 and older" (p. xiv), from which one could extrapolate that by 2010, fully one-quarter of today's academic librarians will retire. Of course, many factors impact an individual's decision to retire; certainly economic, political, and societal issues may impact entire groups of people's decisions to retire so only time will tell how accurate Wilder's predictions are. Wilder explains that retirements in the near future may affect certain segments of library work more than others, with cataloging predicted to be particularly hard hit: "16% of ARL catalogers were age 60 and over in 2000, compared with 10% of the overall ARL population; 32% [of ARL catalogers] were age 55 and over, almost twice as many as in the reference population" (p. xv). What has come to be known as the "graying" of librarians may well affect cataloging sooner than it affects public service, but all specializations are likely to be affected as time goes by. One factor affecting the age of librarians is the comparatively older age of MLS students, compared with other professional programs (p. 18) and one way to counter the aging of the librarian population is to encourage "first career" individuals to pursue the MLS or otherwise choose a career in libraries. Clearly, library student workers are an untapped population of potential recruits. All library professionals have a responsibility for recruitment, and student library assistants, particularly those who perform well and enjoy their jobs, are often prime candidates for full-time library work or for library school.

> Approach each task as a learning opportunity for the student. Perhaps he or she is learning how to use the library or perhaps learning tolerance for his or her least favorite part of a job—both are important learning experiences.

MYTHS ABOUT THE DISADVANTAGES OF HIRING STUDENT ASSISTANTS

Time and time again, colleagues remark that student workers, being such a transient population, do not have much to offer us. Having been burned by student workers who quit after a short time, they complain that it is a waste of time to invest so much work in recruiting and training "temporary" workers. Many library managers are of the attitude that student workers are expendable and don't treat them very well. While there are definitely ways to turn these disadvantage myths around, there is also some kernel of truth to each of them and ways to prevent some of the common problems of managing students.

STUDENTS CANNOT SOLVE ALL YOUR PROBLEMS

I want a ready-trained student worker. Should I hire a library school intern?

Since every library's policies and workflows are unique, there, unfortunately, is no such thing as a ready-trained student worker. Interns can be great for more specialized jobs, particularly on short-term projects. But, don't forget what a huge responsibility it is to hire an intern. Before you hire an intern, think carefully about what the job offers them. An internship should provide the intern with many learning opportunities. Supervising an intern takes a lot more work to do properly, so proceed with caution.

Unfortunately, hiring student workers is not a magical answer to all of your department's staffing problems. While it may be easier to obtain funding for student positions than it is to obtain funding for regular, full-time positions, it can still be an uphill battle to obtain funding for any job. Additionally, having an effective student worker program is a tremendous amount of work, although the work, if done properly, certainly has a tremendous pay-off. However, student assistants are a much less expensive type of staff. Their hourly wages are usually lower and they don't require fringe benefits. While centralized campus Human Resources, compensation and budget offices may need to approve new full-time jobs or even minor changes to existing jobs, student assistant positions can usually be created simply with approval from within the library and job changes may not require any approval at all.

STUDENTS CREATE MORE INITIAL WORK

Creating a student position requires you to think through department needs carefully and document all of the details to justify spending resources on student staffing lines. You will need to define the job and related expectations clearly, and you may find that you are relaying expectations to someone who may never have had a job before. You will need to develop effective training materials. Recruitment, especially effective recruitment, can be time-consuming, and you'll need to trust yourself to make smart hiring decisions. It will be necessary to invest time and effort to ensure that student workers are properly trained and oriented. And after all of that, the real work of day-to-day supervision, continual training, and coaching begins! But, careful selection can increase retention, so the more time you invest in a quality recruitment effort, the less often you will have to repeat it. The better trained a student is, the more likely he or she is to derive satisfaction from the job. The better oriented they are, the more likely they are to feel comfortable in their workplace. Recruitment, training, and orientation are all investments in greater retention of student staff.

STUDENTS ARE NOT WORTH THE TIME INVESTMENT

The common misconception held by many supervisors, that student workers are "flaky" and it is not worth the time and effort to train them, does have a kernel of truth at its center. A supervisor can do much to reduce drastically if not eliminate this flakiness; however, in minimally organized student worker programs students have gotten away with poor performance and poor attendance. If performance standards in the department are low, students will not perform well. Some effort is required to hold workers to high standards, but by clearly explaining expectations and monitoring performance, serious performance issues can be avoided. Being organized, fair, and flexible, and by communicating with students, you can greatly reduce absenteeism and other flaky behavior. Because work to a student is a responsibility secondary to school, students haven't always kept their commitment to part-time campus jobs.

HOW TO DISPEL THE MYTHS

Two things will work in your favor against these common misconceptions. First, the Millennial Generation, the children of Baby Boomers likely to peak in high school graduation numbers in 2008, are very different from the generations that came before them (Woodall, 2004: 59). As a group, this generation trusts authority, values commitment to institutions, and follows the rules (DeBard, 2004: 40). Hence, it follows that members of this generation are likely to be very loyal workers, even to part-time jobs. Second, the more time and energy you put into planning and executing your student worker program, the greater the chance that you will experience positive results in the attendance, performance, and retention of the students you employ. Having an effective student worker program is a fair amount of work, but the payoff in productivity and retention can be tremendous.

The idea of hiring a library school student intern can be an attractive proposition. Unlike rank-and-file university students who may obtain a job in the library purely for some pocket money, or perhaps for some workplace exposure, library school students come to us with (at the very least) an appreciation for library work and (hopefully) some knowledge about library tasks. As with all aspects of library management, there is a tradeoff involved in employing a library school student, particularly if that person is an unpaid intern receiving academic credit for the experience. Interns are not simply free labor. Hosting an intern is a serious commitment, as the internship must fulfill an educational role that is more concrete than that for other student workers. Hosting an intern requires careful planning to ensure that interns are adequately challenged, they are performing tasks that meet departmental needs, and they are learning skills and concepts that will help to prepare them for their careers. Supervising interns can be a highly rewarding experience but it takes a tremendous amount of work to do it properly.

Figure 1-1. Hosting Interns vs. Hiring Students

HONING EFFECTIVE MANAGEMENT SKILLS

Now that you are convinced that there really is no downside to having a well-run student worker program, the question arises: How do you manage them effectively? Frequently, new or recently promoted librarians and library staff are introduced to administration by taking on responsibility for managing student workers. They may have had little or no exposure to management concepts and little or no human resources management experience. Where should they begin?

In many cases, managing student workers is not that different from managing anyone else. Good management is good management, regardless of the demographic of manager and staff. Thinking generally, the three most important aspects of management are effective communication, staying organized, and tapping into motivation. If you can master keeping yourself, the work, and the staff organized while being a good listener and keeping staff informed of any changes, you will be on your way to being an effective manager.

> 1. Communicate Clearly
> 2. Organize Constantly
> 3. Motivate Specifically
>
> **Figure 1-2. Critical Management Skills**

COMMUNICATE CLEARLY

Successful communication results in higher morale, steady productivity, and reduced workplace stress for everyone involved (Moeller-Peifer, 1992: 43). Communication is especially important and especially challenging with student assistants as they tend to have disparate work schedules (Slagell and Langendorfer, 2003: 280). Effective communication involves explaining goals and objectives to the staff, so that they understand the context of management decisions. It includes conducting staff meetings to keep them on the right track. Scheduling a staff meeting around the class schedules of a large group can be quite a challenge, but is not impossible. Schedule meetings at a time when no classes are in session, perhaps on a Friday afternoon, a weekend, or evening. You may also need to conduct the same staff meeting at two separate times to make sure everyone can attend at least one meeting.

Managers' Roundtable Discussion

Question: What is the number one, most important skill needed for managing student workers?

Scott: Communication. I think it's important to communicate your expectations to the students and have them understand that this is a real job and that their contribution is important to the overall mission of the library. I often make the point that the job can go on their résumé and that I'm willing to act as a reference for them. I also recognize that they are here to go to school, so I ask them to communicate clearly with me when they need to make adjustments in their schedules. Flexibility might be the second most important skill.

Werner: The ability to make the work engaging for students is very important. One technique I have used is to give them assignments where they need to determine the method for producing a certain result. This can give them a sense of ownership about a project.

Bonnie: Balancing authority with camaraderie. To do this, I view them through lens of the future professional they will become. I listen to their suggestions, and have implemented some of the good ideas that students have come up with. But, I'm also firm on the fact that written policy is not up for discussion; that it exists for real reasons and must be enforced whether or not a student worker agrees with it. Establishing camaraderie requires an intuitive approach. I've learned to read their faces and to ease into discussions with students so as not to overwhelm them. Thoughtful gestures, like pizza parties, giving them small holiday gifts, and generally providing a nurturing atmosphere also help.

Conni: Actually, it's a blend of two qualities: firmness and compassion. You have to be willing to hold your student assistants accountable, which means sometimes you have to correct them or even fire them. You also have to be compassionate, care about them and enjoy their company, and give them a chance to tell their side of the story even when you are not going to change your mind. Being very structured, principle oriented, and organized doesn't hurt, either.

Michael: The ability and willingness to provide a full and thorough training on all tasks that are involved in the student's work responsibility is the most important skill when managing student workers.

Gary: It's easy to think of student employees as employees. They are not. I have to remind myself often that I have students working for me. Yes, they are employees but their main job is to be a student. It is also my role to educate them on how the working world outside of academia will treat them.

Nick: The most important skill for me is to be well organized. I plan ahead as much as possible, so that I'm not scrambling about when a new term begins.

Question: How much does a supervisor of student assistants need to know about the Federal Work Study Program?

Scott: I know very little about the Federal Work Study Program. The only thing I really need to know is whether or not they are eligible. We do encourage students to go to the work study office to check, in case they aren't sure of their award of eligibility.

Werner: In previous positions, I never needed to know much about the program much beyond what our budget was.

Bonnie: At my institution, we need to know the deadline to apply for work study each year and make sure our students apply before the deadline. We also need to know the hours per week/per month limits for work study and how many hours students must be enrolled in to qualify for work study. Lastly, we need to show students how to fill out timesheets to meet work study criteria.

(Cont'd.)

Managers' Roundtable Discussion *(Continued)*

Conni: Fortunately, I don't have to know much about work study—only the limit on hours/week students can work. We have an excellent personnel staff who take care of the process for us.

Michael: Here at Queens, I need to know very little about work study. All of our student hiring is done centrally, so students just show up at our door with a set amount of hours for the academic year. Students are responsible for keeping track of the hours they were granted. Otherwise, if they are deemed reliable and want more work they can be further employed and funded with available temporary services funding.

Gary: I need to know very little about the Federal Work Study Program. I could not explain in detail much about the program.

Nick: The work study program will only subsidize their wage for a set number of hours over the course of the year so I must track their hours. Once these hours are used up, these students become SAs (where we pay their full wage). In order to minimize our costs, I try to schedule these students so that their hours will last us for the complete academic year. This may mean that they will work less hours per week than an SA.

Scott Hanscom, Johns Hopkins University
Werner Haun, Library of Congress
Bonnie Hines, Louisiana State University of Alexandria
Conni Kitten, Texas Tech University Libraries

Michael Miller, Queens College—City University of New York
Gary Ploski, Sarah Lawrence College
Nick Rizzo, University of British Columbia

> If you think you need to improve your management skills, focus on improving your personal organization and communication skills.

Communication means reminding staff of little-used policy and keeping them abreast of any policy changes. It means regular e-mail contact and announcements as well as in-person "news briefs," utilizing technology such as blogs or course software, and prompt corrective conversations. It means delegating confidently and unapologetically, and following up with staff to whom you have delegated tasks or projects. When delegating, do not feel that you are imposing on staff. Remember that it is your responsibility to get your department's work done, and there is no way that you can accomplish it all yourself. You must delegate most of the work to the departmental staff, both full-time staff and students, to perform your department's primary functions. Your role is to hire right, train well, assign tasks fairly, and follow up to be sure that work is completed correctly.

Perhaps, most importantly, communication means listening to suggestions that staff have for improving departmental processes and creating opportunities for staff to ask questions. When it comes to improving service to patrons, improving service to colleagues, or improving workflow, front-line staff are in a position to make well-informed suggestions. However, many staff will be reluctant to make suggestions without specifically being invited to do so. The same goes for asking clarifying questions of you. Many staff members will feel intimidated by asking you to clarify instructions or explain policies unless they are specifically asked to do so. Make listening a priority and create many opportunities to listen.

Students who are part of the Millennial Generation respond well to structured situations with rules. Generation X workers, those born 1965–1980, who, though slightly older than Millennials, may still be part of your student workforce, prefer less structure and more learning by trial and error (*Techniques*, 2003: 51). One of the most important guidelines of any type of communication is to know your audience, so exploring the generational affiliations of your student staff, as well as their own personal communication styles, will be extremely helpful in planning effective communication.

Five Elements of Effective Communication

There are five elements to keep in mind to ensure that your communication is effective, as outlined by Kathleen Moeller-Peifer in the "Communication" chapter of Joan Geiseke's useful book, *Practical Help for New Supervisors* (1992). They are:

1. Plan your communication. Think about the 5 W's—the who, what, when, where, and why you need to get across. Choose the appropriate method of communication. It may be better to make the rounds and tell everyone in person if you want to make sure everyone receives the information. If the information is complicated or otherwise may be something staff wish to refer back to, it may be better to e-mail the information or post it to a staff blog, Internet site, or at each workstation. In most departments, a combination of communication methods with careful choices, depending on the information you need to convey, works best.

2. Communicate accurate information. Before you pass any information along, be sure you are giving the correct information. If you are not certain the information you have is accurate, you should wait until you have received confirmation on its accuracy before you communicate it to anyone.

3. Communicate clearly and concisely. Be sure you do not provide too much information, or otherwise present the information in a confusing way.

4. Communicate appropriate and relevant information. Know your audience and communicate the right information to the right group. Staff are generally concerned with information related to the future of the organization, working conditions, daily operations, and job requirements. When communicating in person, be sure the body language you convey is appropriate.

I don't feel like a very effective manager. I'm running around like a headless chicken while the students who work in my department spend their time instant messaging their friends and surfing the Web. How can I become a better manager?

The first step to take is to look at your own organizational skills. Managing people takes planning, and if you aren't organized, it's hard not to be in crisis mode. Take a deep breath and get organized! Keep a list of what you need to accomplish, and review your list daily, asking yourself, "What is it I must do, and what could possibly be done by someone else?" It will take some effort to train others to do the work and to review that work, but that's a much better use of your time than doing everything yourself.

5. Listen to responses. This guideline is listed last because it generally happens after you have shared information, not because it is any less important than the other elements of effective communication. It is essential to give employees some time to respond to what you have said. Don't immediately walk away after sharing information, but give everyone time to digest and ask follow-up questions. Once you have shared the information the first time, bring up the issue again in another forum to provide ample opportunity for employees to ask for clarification.

ORGANIZE CONSTANTLY

Stay organized and communicate clearly.

There are as many ways to be organized as there are managers. It's not important that you need to get organized according to any specific philosophy or program, but simply that you get organized! As a manager, you will have multiple projects and responsibilities going on, and without committing to some organizational strategies you simply will not be successful. It is vitally important that you have trusted a system where you record your obligations, which means some type of calendar and some type of to-do list. Some managers prefer to trust a paper system, while others prefer some variant of an electronic system. It is important to manage your time and responsibilities and to keep the deluge of information that you receive on a daily basis in some sort of order. Perhaps the only situation more stressful than feeling disorganized and out of control is having a supervisor who is disorganized. Keep in mind how your personal organization impacts others in your department and make it a priority.

Five Tips for Staying Organized

1. Keep a calendar. It does not matter if you choose a paper or electronic calendar; what matters is you choose one calendar and use it religiously.
2. Keep a to-do list. Be sure you record everything you have to do and refer back to your list. Your to-do list may include long-range projects as well as short-range tasks.
3. Set aside time to do what you have to do. Your calendar is essential not only for remembering appointments and meetings that you are obligated to attend, but it is also your key to getting things done. By blocking out time on your calendar and making "appointments" with

yourself to do what is required of you, you will ensure that items on your to-do list actually get done.

4. Check your e-mail on a schedule. E-mail is simultaneously the best efficiency tool of the century and the biggest time-waster and distraction. Check your e-mail three or four times per day, rather than every five seconds. If your e-mail has an auditory signal as messages come in, turn it off. If you read a message that you can take care of in two minutes or less, take care of it immediately, then file or delete the message. For those items that will take more time, set aside time on your calendar for addressing them.

5. Keep a written record of what you have delegated. By noting what you have delegated and to whom, you will be able to follow up more efficiently. Noting when you need to follow up on a calendar is helpful, or simply keeping a list of the items you are waiting for can help to ensure these items are not forgotten.

RECOGNIZE GENERATIONAL WORK STYLES AND MOTIVATORS

True motivation comes from within an employee and can't be dictated, but you can certainly help to create an environment that makes it easy for people to be motivated. One way to do this is to understand what is important to the people that you supervise. When managing anyone remember his or her perspective. For example, the students that you supervise are students first and foremost, and their main priority is their education. By being respectful of this reality, you can ensure that your workers give you the best effort they possibly can. Stressing the benefits of their library job (such as what they can learn and how it can help them to be better students now and better workers in the future) is one way to keep them interested. Another way to plug into a worker's motivation is to know what is important to him or her. Lately, much has been written about the different motivators and workstyles of the four generations—Traditionalists, Baby Boomers, Generation X, and Millennials—in today's workplace.

Traditionalists, also known as the Silent Generation, were born between 1900 and 1945. Traditionalists tend to favor book learning and are generally loyal to the workplace, hardworking, frugal, and conservative. They are most comfortable with traditional gender roles and, since many men of this generation served in the military, they are comfortable with a top-down chain of command style of management (Wilson and Folz, 2005: 55).

Baby Boomers, born between 1946 and 1964, are inner driven and competitive (hey, what would you expect from the largest generation our

> **I've been trying to delegate, but I have trouble remembering who is doing what, and what deadlines I gave them. Am I losing my mind?**
>
> Of course not. You're just really busy. Make it easier on yourself by keeping a written record of the assignments you have given, the dates you made the assignments, and the dates you must follow up on them. Review this list every day. It's also helpful to keep track of the deadlines you assign by writing them on your calendar.

country has ever seen? They came of age as 80 million well-educated youngsters, competing for the same jobs). Boomers, who grew up with the new invention of television, tend to be optimistic idealists who trust themselves rather than authority. While they like teamwork, the competition they are used to can sometimes derail their best efforts in a team setting. They are goal and results oriented. Unlike the traditionalists, they are cynical of loyalty. As they are confident of their own abilities, they are likely to be content with the traditional annual evaluation (Wilson and Folz, 2005: 55–56; DeBard, 2004: 40).

Generation X, born between 1965 and 1980, are also known as the Thirteenth Generation and, numbering 46 million, are a much smaller group than the Baby Boomers. Generation X grew up with a high rate of divorced parents and a large percentage of working mothers. These were the "latchkey kids" of the 1970s and 1980s and, as a result, they are "street smart free agents" (DeBard 2004: 166). They are independent workers who don't trust authority, consider loyalty naïve, and admire creating enterprise. They function well in creative environments not bound by rules, and are loyal to projects and teams as opposed to companies. Generation X does not function well with controlling management styles and generally wants space to do their jobs. They appreciate authenticity and are unimpressed by authority. The recession and downsizing they lived through as children and adolescents produced a conservative economic outlook in them as adults. They strive for a good work-life balance and work for them is simply a means to an end, not an end in itself. More experience-oriented and less materialistic than Baby Boomers, they strive for a balanced life and see work as a means to fund their experiences outside of work. They crave feedback and will ask for it reluctantly, but do not generally take criticism well (Wilson and Folz, 2005: 56–58; DeBard, 2004: 40; Legault, 2003: 23).

The Millennials, born between 1981 and 1999, are the children of the Baby Boomers. Also known as the Echo Boomers, Generation Y, Generation Next, and the Next Generation, they represent the largest cohort since the Boomers. Millennials are outer-driven team players who exhibit good followership. This culturally diverse group trusts authority, is intensely loyal and, having been given awards for participation in a way that other generations were not, desires continual feedback. These were the kids who grew up protected, with "baby on board" signs on the family car. Their childhoods were characterized by structured group play, and, as a result, they function well in an environment of structure and rules, and expect a team-based approach at work. They have known technology all their lives and are comfortable with multitasking. Millennials appreciate diversity and collaboration, and like being friends with their coworkers. Similarly, they recognize they can't learn everything from one person; hence, they appreciate having a variety of mentors and appreciate learning from a variety of situations. They generally expect to have part-time jobs and internships while in school, and value these as learning experiences on a par with classroom work (Legault, 2003: 24; Howe and Strauss, 2000: 166; Wilson and Folz, 2005: 56; Lancaster and Stillman, 2003: 34; DeBard, 2004: 33–35, 40; Marshall, 2004: 18).

Generationally speaking, it is most likely that the student assistants that you supervise are part of the Millennial Generation. Just as each generation before them, Millennials were shaped by their experiences, including the competitive nature of their Baby-Boom parents. By learning about the expectations of the people you supervise, you can be better prepared to tap into those expectations for motivational purposes. Since an increasing percentage of college students are not-traditionally aged (Oblinger, 2003: 38), it is still common to encounter members of Generation X as student assistants. Think about the generational identity of everyone in your area and determine how best to assign people to work together.

> **How do I know what will motivate my student assistants to do a good job?**
>
> Generally, creating an interesting work environment, where staff are treated kindly and fairly, is a good start. Beyond that, ask them.

WORKING WITH THE FEDERAL WORK STUDY PROGRAM

Federal Work Study is one type of financial aid that students at the undergraduate and master's levels may receive. In exchange for services provided, students earn money to help pay for education expenses. Work Study is one of the most commonly awarded types of financial aid and has advantages for both recipients and employers.

> **My institution allows me to hire only work study students. How can I ensure I get good workers?**
>
> While theoretically your applicant pool might be limited in numbers if only work study students can apply, you can ensure quality by writing an attractive job advertisement or communicating your needs clearly to the department that does hiring at your institution. Careful screening and reference checking will also help you to select appropriate candidates.

VIEW THE PROGRAM FROM THE STUDENT'S PERSPECTIVE

Students must apply for financial aid annually, using the Free application for Student Aid, or FAFSA, available on the Web at www.fafsa.edu.gov. Work study is one type of financial aid that a student may receive. In exchange for work provided on campus, students receive wages to partially defray the cost of education. On some campuses, libraries only hire students with work study awards, while on other campuses libraries may hire a mix of work study and non-work study students. Since a student's financial aid package is based on financial need as determined by the school's financial aid office, each student receives a different dollar amount of federal work study funds which is used to pay a portion—50–80 percent—of his or her wages until it is exhausted. Depending on local policies, a student's work study award may dictate how many hours can be worked per week during the school year, so as not to exhaust the funds prematurely. Once funds are used, students may be separated or continued, depending on local practices.

VIEW THE PROGRAM FROM THE MANAGER'S PERSPECTIVE

As work study awards are based on need, each student will receive a different dollar amount of Federal Work Study. These funds are used to pay a portion of the student's wages, so that the department effectively retains the student at a discount hourly wage. Once the student's work study award is exhausted, he or she can only be retained in the department if the department is willing to pay his or her entire hourly wage. Managers may be required to track spending of financial aid awards to ensure that student staff do not exhaust them prematurely, prior to the end of the school year.

EMBRACING YOUR MANAGEMENT RESPONSIBILITIES

Campus jobs are part of a student's education. It is our job to teach students how to work, as much as it is our job to teach them how to do the specific work that is assigned. Just as it is extremely rare for a student to accept a library job knowing much, if anything, about library work, students may not know much about conducting themselves in any workplace. It is our responsibility to teach them about job expectations, as well as teach them the job skills necessary to get the job done. Generally, Millennial students are predisposed to following the rules, but it is our responsibility as supervisors to clearly articulate those rules (DeBard, 2004: 36). To Millennials, knowledge in and of itself is not the ultimate goal. They value practicality and applicable skills, and therefore are drawn to internships and part-time jobs in college as a way to meet this need. This desire for learning means that supervisors must make part-time jobs meaningful to potential student workers, both for recruitment and retention. Figure 1-3 capsulizes some management basics.

Simply put, management is getting things done through other people. Less simply put, management has several facets, including supervision, planning, staffing, measuring, and improving. Supervision includes monitoring staff to ensure they get the work done within accepted standards. Planning includes thinking strategically to determine what improvements will need to be made down the line. Staffing refers to everything involved with ensuring that we have an appropriate number of effective workers to get the job done. Measuring and improving deal with collecting and using data to improve our processes. Bad management can include characteristics such as micro-managing, not listening, having unrealistic expectations, showing signs of burnout, or simply not being personable. Good management is a little bit more difficult to pinpoint, but you know it when you see

> As a supervisor, be *friendly* but not *friends* with those who report to you.

A good manager tries always to . . .	A good manager tries never to . . .
Communicate well	Assume everyone "hears" the same way
Trust and be trustworthy	Act moody or dishonest
Act engaged	Shirk responsibility
Stay organized	Avoid keeping organized
Plan strategically	Get bogged down in the nuts and bolts
Become knowledgeable	Make decisions without knowing all the facts
Lead enthusiastically	Seem fearful to make unpopular decisions
Treat staff fairly	Show favoritism
Project stablity	Fly off the handle
Act friendly	Be a friend

Figure 1-3. Characteristics of Good and Bad Management

it. If you are lucky, you have witnessed an excellent manager in action. Even the best managers, however, make their share of mistakes, and those mistakes can be valuable learning tools for anyone who is paying attention and thinking about how to avoid them in his or her own career.

KNOW AND USE SUPPORT SYSTEMS

As a supervisor, it is your responsibility to know the human resources policies of your library, college, or university. It is important to be familiar with any responsibilities you may have for the welfare of the students you supervise *before* there is a problem. Talk to your supervisor or human resources representative about what your role is, for example, if you suspect a student worker is having a problem with drugs or alcohol. Similarly, ask what to do if a student brings personal problems to work or if you otherwise suspect he or she may be depressed or the victim of physical violence. It's important to know the scope of social services offered to students at your institution and to obtain information on how to make appropriate referrals. It is of paramount importance to know what your obligations and limitations are regarding getting involved with these issues.

Every morning after "party nights" students under my supervision seem listless, and, frankly, hung-over. How can I respect the indulgences of their youth and still get the best possible work from them?

Keep in mind the standards for the job. If employees are not meeting agreed upon workplace expectations for performance, then you need to take corrective action. Focus on the job requirements that are not being met, not the partying that you suspect occurred the night before. Investigate your campus policies regarding substance use. As a professional at the institution, it may be your responsibility to report suspected substance abuse problems, underage drinking, or drug use. Being intoxicated on the job is another issue to watch out for, and something that results in immediate termination in most workplaces.

All institutions of higher learning have some degree of student support. Talk to people at your institution to get a rough idea of the scope of the dean of students, health center, counseling center, housing office, registrar, judicial boards, student employment office, women's center, office of international students, and any other specialized services.

CONCLUSION

Since student assistants became part of the library workforce at the beginning of the twentieth century, there has been an increasing reliance on them for more and more specialized library work. Today we rely on the contribution of student workers throughout the library to compare essential tasks and functions. Through their library employment, students learn both about libraries and about workplaces in general. Because of their exposure to library work, some student assistants may choose to pursue careers in libraries. Managing students well is one way to keep them satisfied in their jobs and reduce employee turnover among your student staff. Good management includes clear, effective communication, optimal organizational skills, and tapping into employee's intrinsic motivation by determining what is important to them, and responding to it.

EXERCISES

EXERCISE 1-1: QUALITIES OF GOOD AND BAD MANAGEMENT

Select a manager with qualities you admire and would try to emulate. Think about what makes him or her a good manager.

1. Write down 5 habits, or actions, or attitudes that you witnessed in this good manager. (Example: He was always fair to employees; she explained procedures clearly.)

   1.

   2.

   3.

    4.

    5.

2. List concrete ways you might incorporate the items listed in #1 into your management routine?

    1.

    2.

    3.

    4.

    5.

3. Now think about the people who have taught you what not to do. What management mistakes have you witnessed? What are you sure you should not ever do?

Write down five habits, actions, or attitudes you have witnessed that you would characterize as poor management.

    1.

    2.

    3.

    4.

    5.

List concrete ways you can be sure not to repeat these mistakes.

    1.

    2.

    3.

    4.

    5.

EXERCISE 1-2: HUMAN RESOURCES AND STUDENT EMPLOYMENT

Make an appointment to talk to your human resources officer. Call the office to determine which member of the HR staff is primarily responsible for issues related to student employment. Ask that person the following questions and note the answers he or she provides:

How do we handle discipline?	
How do we handle poor performance?	
What documentation procedures do I need to follow when taking corrective action or disciplining a student employee?	
What do I do if I suspect a student is under the influence of drugs or alcohol?	
What do I do if I suspect abuse?	

EXERCISE 1-3: INVESTIGATING CAMPUS RESOURCES

Investigate the various student service offices at your institution to determine how they assist students. Make a note of how to contact them, the services they offer, and how to refer students when necessary.

Office	Phone	Services Offered	Referral Process
Dean of Students			
Health Center			
Housing Office			
Registrar			
Judicial Board(s)			
Student Employment			
Women's Center			
Office of International Students			
Counseling Center			

REFERENCES

Association of Research Libraries. *ARL Statistics: Interactive Edition.* www.fisher.lib.virginia.edu/arl.

Burrows, Janice. "Training Student Workers in Academic Libraries: How and Why?" *Journal of Library Administration* 21, 3/4 (1995): 77–86.

Dawes, Trevor, Kimberly Burke Sweetman, and Catherine Von Elm. *Access Services* (SPEC Kit 290). Washington, DC: Association of Research Libraries, 2005.

DeBard, Michael. "Millennials Coming to College." *New Directions for Student Services* 106 (Summer 2004): 33–45.

Dermody, Melinda, and Susan Schleper. "Supervising: What They Didn't Teach You in Library School." *College and Research Libraries News* 65 (June 2004): 306–308, 332.

DesJardins, Stephen L., Dennis Ahlburg, and Brian P. McCall. "An Event History Model of Student Departure." *Economics of Education Review* 18 (1999): 375–390.

DesJardins, Stephen L., Dennis Ahlburg, and Brian P. McCall. "A Temporal Investigation of Factors Related to Timely Degree Completion." *Journal of Higher Education* 73 (September/October 2002): 555–581.

Epstein, Carmen. "Using Blackboard for Training and Communicating with Student Employees." *College and Undergraduate Libraries* 10, 1 (2003): 21–25.

Gregory, David. "The Evolving Role of Student Employees in Academic Libraries." *Journal of Library Administration* 21, 3/4 (1995): 3–27.

Howe, Neil, and William Strauss. *Millennials Rising: The Next Great Generation.* New York: Vintage Books, 2000.

Kerkvliet, Joe, and Clifford Nowell. "Does One Size Fit All? University Differences in the Influence of Wages, Financial Aid and Integration on Student Retention." *Economics of Education Review* 24 (2005): 89–95.

Lancaster, Lynne, and David Stillman. "From World War II to the World Wide Web: Traditionalists, Baby Boomers Generation Xers and Millennials at Work." *Women in Business* 55 (November/December 2003): 33–36.

Legault, Marie. "Caution: Mixed Generations at Work." *Canadian HR Reporter* 16, 21(December 1, 2003): 23–24.

Marshall, Jeffrey. "Managing Different Generations at Work." *Financial Executive* 20, 5 (July/August 2004): 18.

Moeller-Peifer, Kathleen. "Communication." In *Practical Help for New Supervisors.* Edited by Joan Geiseke. Chicago: American Library Association, 1992.

Oblinger, Diana. "Boomers, GenXers & Millennials: Understanding the New Students." *EDUCAUSE Review* 38 (July-August 2003): 37–47.

Slagell, Jeff, and Jeanne Langendorfer. "Don't Tread on Me: The Art of Supervising Student Assistants." *The Serials Librarian* 44 (2003): 279–284.

Systems, Procedures and Exchange Center, Association of Research Libraries. *Student Employment in ARL Libraries* (Kit 168). Washington, DC: ARL, 1990.

"*Techniques* Interviews Author Neil Howe About Millennials in the Workplace." *Techniques* 76, 6 (Spring 2003): 51.

United States Department of Education. Office of Educational Research and Improvement. National Center for Education Statistics. *The Status of Academic Libraries in the United States: Results from the 1996 Academic Library Survey with Historical Comparisons.* Prepared by Maggie Cahalan, Wendy Mansfield, and Natalie Justh. NCES 2001-301. Washington, DC: U.S. Department of Education, May 2001.

Wilder, Stanley. *Age Demographics of Librarians: A Profession Apart.* Washington, D.C.: Association of Research Libraries, 1995.

Wilder, Stanley. *Demographic Change in Academic Librarianship.* Washington, D.C.: Association of Research Libraries, 2003.

Wilson, Christine, and John Folz. "Managing Multiple Generations at Work." *Feed and Grain* 44 (August/September 2005): 54–60.

Woodall, David. "Enter the Millennials." *Prism* 13 (Summer 2004): 59.

2 PREPARING TO RECRUIT STUDENT ASSISTANTS

WHY SPEND TIME PREPARING?

Thoroughly preparing your recruitment efforts ensures that they will go smoothly and produce the results you need. By documenting your need for additional help, you will be able to make a solid argument for the additional funding required. Analyzing the workflow will also allow you to adjust processes to make your department more efficient. Thorough preparation for recruiting ensures that you design a job that groups together a reasonable array of tasks for a student assistant. Writing an accurate job description and clearly defining job competencies will help you to hire the right person for the job.

ESTABLISHING THE NEED

Whether you already employ some student assistants and are looking for ways to improve you student-worker operation or you are simply considering hiring student-workers to increase your department's efficiency, some planning and preparation are essential to building up a successful student employment program within your department. Five steps to prepare for recruitment include:

1. Identify the need (What tasks need to get done? What do you hope to accomplish?)
2. Identify what can be eliminated or streamlined (Could your goals be accomplished by adjusting departmental workflow or assigning tasks differently?)
3. Design the job (Which tasks are appropriate for student-worker[s]? Which are more appropriate for full-time staff, supervisors, or librarians?)

4. Obtain approval for student hires (Who must endorse your plan to hire students?)

5. Secure funding for student hires (How do you get a budget line to pay for new student hires? What approval is necessary?).

Even before you begin to recruit student workers, you need to plan for recruitment, which begins by examining departmental needs. If you have never had a student worker in the position you are considering, the first step in hiring a student is determining whether or not you need one. Certainly, you would not have picked up this book if you didn't think that hiring one or more student workers was a good direction for your department, but be sure that hiring additional people is absolutely necessary. The more people you manage, the more complex your own job is, and you do not want to add complexity to your job responsibilities unless it is absolutely necessary. Furthermore, you will need to justify your decision to the person or people who control the funds at your organization, and these people will want cold, hard facts to justify spending additional money. You'll need to convince them that you have thought through the issue completely, and that there is no way around spending additional money for one or more student assistants. To determine if additional hires are necessary, conduct a comprehensive departmental workflow audit, which includes a thorough analysis of all jobs and an analysis of workflow. The workflow audit will help to identify work that can be done more efficiently or perhaps even eliminated.

> **I'm desperate for students and don't have time to plan. Do I really need to go through all these planning steps?**
>
> The short answer is *yes*, because you must convince whomever controls the budget that funding is needed for these positions. But, if you have already come to the conclusion yourself, it may be quite easy to make that case.

EXAMINING WORKFLOW TO STREAMLINE OR ELIMINATE WORK EFFORTS

Simply put, workflow is how you do what you do. Workflow is the list of tasks involved in accomplishing your department's primary aims and how these tasks relate to one another. It is what W. Edwards Deming would call a "system": the work practices, or steps, involved in accomplishing your primary aim. Deming (2005) asserted that, since workplace performance is governed by these systems, individual workers are only as good as the system in which they are working. Thus, if the workflows in place are not efficient, there is no way that workers can be efficient (Deming, 2005).

The workflow audit consists of two primary steps: identifying all workflows in the department and identifying all of the steps involved in each workflow. For example, a reference department might have the following workflows:

1. Answering questions at the reference desk
2. Assisting users with technical or database questions at computers
3. Keeping all printed guides, pencils, and scrap paper available in the reference room.

A copy cataloging department would have different workflows:

1. Searching for cataloging copy
2. Routing books requiring original cataloging to the appropriate department
3. Labeling newly cataloged material.

A computer desktop support department will have still different workflows:

1. Answering calls and logging problems into a tracking database
2. Installing new software
3. Installing new hardware.

Next, identify all of the steps involved with each departmental workflow and who performs each step. Once you have determined all of the steps, you will find it helpful to draw a process map, or flowchart, that represents the system of your work. If your work processes are particularly long or complicated, it is helpful to divide long processes into shorter ones to make flowcharting easier and more detailed (Martin, 2004: 205).

For example, let's say that you are the manager of a busy reference department. In the past two months you have seen three comments in the suggestion box referring to the lack of pencils and scrap paper for patrons to jot down call numbers and citations. Yesterday, your boss also forwarded an angry e-mail on this topic from a professor in the English department. The funny thing is that the department *does* provide pencils and scrap paper, so you investigate the situation. You immediately restock all pencils and paper, as well as the pathfinder guides that you notice are low. Two days later, you notice that, once again, scrap paper and pencils are nowhere to be found. You may think to yourself, "I'm much too busy to take on this important task, but perhaps we could hire a student worker to help us with some of these important support functions here in Reference."

SAMPLE WORKFLOW ANALYSIS: KEEPING STOCKS SUPPLIED

Is this hire really necessary? To find out, take a look at the workflow. You identify the following steps involved with keeping supplies stocked:

Step	Person Responsible
Check pencil and scrap paper supply at workstations and Reference desk	No one assigned; currently not done consistently
Refill pencils and scrap paper from supply cabinet	No one assigned; currently not done consistently
Check stock of paper pathfinder guides	No one assigned; currently not done consistently
Print out and restock paper pathfinder guides	No one assigned; currently not done consistently
Place supply orders	Joe

Is it any wonder this task isn't getting done consistently? No one is assigned to it. Figure 2-1 shows a process map, which is a graphical way to look at this workflow.

SAMPLE ASSESSMENT OF WORKFLOW OPTIONS

As a manager, you have seen a problem that needs to be addressed, and one solution could be to hire a student to take care of stocking supplies in the Reference room. However, there may be other solutions, perhaps better ones; hence, further investigation is warranted. To help you think about your options, try to answer the following questions:

1. What functions does the department carry out (workflows)?
2. What are the steps we currently perform for each function?
3. Who does what (the "who" can be the job title, especially if more than one person carries out the task, or the actual person)?
4. What is the reason for each step?
5. What could we simply stop doing?
6. If we stopped doing X, what would we need to do to prepare?
7. What isn't working?

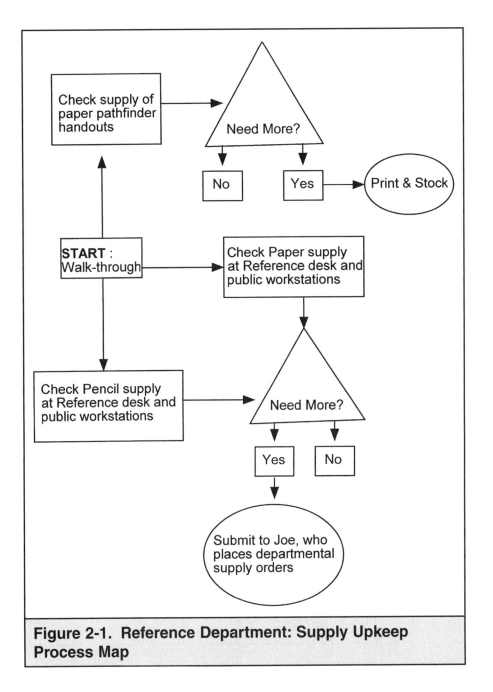

Figure 2-1. Reference Department: Supply Upkeep Process Map

8. What could be done better?

9. How can automation help us?

10. Who has time in their day to take care of (some or all of) this?

For purposes of our example, the answers might look like this:

1. What functions does the department carry out (workflows)?	a. Answering questions at the Reference desk b. Assisting users with technical or database questions at computers c. Keeping all printed guides, pencils, scrap paper available in the Reference room.
2. What are the steps we currently perform for each function? (Here I'm illustrating only those functions associated with workflow #3, but all functions should be written out).	a. Check pencil and scrap paper supply at workstations and Reference desk b. Refill pencils and scrap paper from supply cabinet c. Check stock of paper pathfinder guides and print out more if needed d. Place supply orders when necessary
3. Who does what (the "who" can be the job title, especially if more than one person carries out the task, or the actual person)?	The problem is that no one is currently assigned to restocking; Joe does the ordering.
What is the reason for each step?	a-b. Restocking pencils and paper—so users can write down call numbers or citations they find while consulting reference librarians or using the research machines in the Reference room c. Restocking pathfinders—pathfinders are provided to help users get started in their research d. Purchasing supplies—to be sure we always have enough pencils and scrap paper.
5. What could we simply stop doing?	Theoretically, we could: a. Stop providing paper and/or pencils and require users to bring their own b. Discontinue creating pathfinder guides c. Discontinue printing pathfinder guides (post to Web?).

6. If we stopped doing X, what would we need to do to prepare?	a. If we stopped providing paper and/or pencils, we'd need to be prepared for:
	
	  1. Looking really cheap
	  2. Being asked for paper and pencils a million times per day
	
	b. Could potentially launch a public relations campaign to protect our image and remind users to bring their own paper and pencils

6. If we stopped doing X, what would we need to do to prepare (*continued*)?	c. If we stopped printing pathfinders, we could post them to the Web (they are already in electronic form) and users could use them online or print them as needed.
	
	We would need to:
	  1. Get them posted to the Web
	  2. Inform users and staff they are now on the Web.

7. What isn't working?	a. Users need pencil and paper and requiring them to ask for it drives both them and us crazy b. Guides should to be available when needed.
8. What could be done better? How?	a. Regular supply checks.
9. How can automation help us?	a. Post guides to the Web.
10. Who has time in their day to take care of (some or all of) this?	a. A job analysis will determine who has the time and skills needed to manage the "posting pathfinders project" b. A job analysis can also help to determine if we need a student to stock supplies, or if an existing member of staff can do it.

Based on answers to these questions, some options for the supply dilemma are:

    A. Stop supplying pencils and paper for users
    B. Joe walks through the Reference room every day and restocks the supplies
    C. Reference manager walks through the Reference room every day and restocks the supplies
    D. Charge a reference librarian with restocking supplies
    E. Post the guides to the Web.

Now let's weigh the options. Ceasing to supply pencils and paper is an extreme measure. After all, the problem is not that you cannot afford to purchase golf pencils and scrap paper or that paper and pencils are not meeting the usage need, it's simply that no one is responsible for ensuring users have an adequate supply. Option A, stop supplying pencil and paper for users, is not the best option. Options B or C, which assign the task to a specific person, make sense, but this all depends on what else Joe and the department manager have on their plates already. It could be that Joe has the time and the willingness to walk through the Reference room once or twice per day to be sure the requisite supplies are in place. The Reference

I notice that many of my students use their work time to do homework. How should I respond to this?

Is homework allowed on the job? Can they reasonably get some homework in without neglecting their responsibilities? There are some library student jobs where homework is entirely permissible. For instance, if there is no other work to be done, students working at a reference, circulation, reserve, or computer help desk can probably be allowed to do homework in between assisting users. However, in departments where assisting users is secondary (or not part of a student's job) homework is not usually an acceptable activity. For instance, students working in ILL or acquisitions don't have "down time" analogous to that of a student at a help desk waiting for the next user who needs assistance. Students who are allowed to do homework at their library jobs should be clearly instructed that homework should be done only after all job-related tasks are complete, and never to the detriment of patron service.

manager may wish to use this task as an opportunity to check in with staff and users and therefore make it a priority, but unless there is another payoff, stocking supplies is not the best use of the Reference manager's time. As option D suggests, there may be someone else in the department who has the time to take this on. The task of stocking supplies may be made simpler by posting pathfinder guides to the Web, provided your organization has the staffing resources (either existing staff or has the money to pay students to complete this task) to invest in the project. Option E has the added benefit of making these guides available remotely, which means that there is a service benefit as well as a staffing benefit to this project (an argument that may resonate with upper management).

WHAT IS A JOB ANALYSIS?

A job analysis is a review of all of the tasks involved in a particular job. To conduct a job analysis, you'll need to observe workers while they perform their jobs, interview them on what they do, and review training manuals, reports, and any other printed material on departmental procedures (Lin and Kleiner, 2004: 108). To get started, ask all employees in the department (student workers as well as staff at all levels) to write up the various tasks involved in their jobs and approximately how much time they spend on each task. Individuals who have never been asked to do this before may find it challenging. One way to help employees get started on their job audits is to ask them to log their time for a week. Another way would be to ask them simply to list the tasks involved in their jobs and assign percentages to each. It's important that you ask all employees to perform their job audit according to the same directions, or be prepared to translate them so that you are able to write up the workflow audit for the entire department in a meaningful way. If half the department provides you with percentages and the other half provides you with hours per week, it may add unnecessary complexities to the job audit. Similarly, all employees should be given clear instructions on the level of detail you desire; otherwise it will be difficult to compare the work demands of various employees.

Regular (non-student) staff should be asked what they do, what could be done better, which parts of the job are the most routine, and which parts of the job they find most satisfying. Student assistants, if currently employed by the department, should be asked what they do and which parts they enjoy and why. By examining the job audits of all staff, you can determine if projects are assigned equitably, if staff are challenged, if students are contributing to the department in a useful way, and possible reasons for high turnover. The job audit will also help you to assess morale among your staff.

Cheryl Martin details the steps she took to audit and subsequently redesign workflow in the Technical Services division at the library at McMaster University in Canada in a chapter in *Innovative Redesign and*

Reorganization of Library Technical Services: Paths for the Future and Case Studies (2004). At the start of the workflow redesign, she identified the goal of improving service, workflow, and communication. Recognizing the magnitude of the potential change, she made staff members responsible for documenting the steps in the workflow and flowcharting the process. The workflow analysis was overseen by a group of three staff members and two supervisors. The group conducted a separate discussion for each workflow, asking themselves what worked well, what the obvious problems were, and thought of possible solutions. The group determined whether or not everyone involved in the system followed the same steps when carrying out a given task. When individual practices differed, the group documented the differences and explored the reasons for them. The changes at McMaster were initiated with a six-month plan for introduction

---

Managers' Roundtable Discussion

Question: What has been your biggest student worker challenge and how did you overcome it?

Scott: My biggest challenge was integrating students into a unit that had previously only used students in a limited way. The perceived difference between "student work" and "staff work" led to tensions during those periods when students' academic schedules made it hard for them to come to work. The staff resented that the students weren't showing up, and felt that they couldn't do their own work because they were filling in for students. Additionally, most of the day-to-day supervision and training of students fell to me, and the staff never really got to know them. I solved this by abolishing student jobs and instead developed a list of tasks that students could assist us in doing. Presented in this way, the staff took greater ownership of every part of the operation, including the training and supervision of students, and the unit became more cohesive. Although I still maintain overall responsibility for the students, my daily burden is greatly lessened now that students and staff work much more closely with one another.

Werner: Probably my biggest student worker challenge has been working with students who had limited English language skills. I often overcame this difficulty by demonstrating various tasks rather than just telling them what to do. Also, manuals and/or other written instructions were helpful, since these students often had good reading comprehension of English.

Bonnie: Lately, the biggest challenge has been getting student workers off their cell phones. I tell them that if they have to make a call they must go to a private area and not hold personal conversations at the Reference desk. I did not ban cell phones, knowing it would be a losing battle. Student worker supervisors need to pick their battles! We had a written policy to keep personal visits to an absolute minimum and extended this to include cell phone conversations. Occasionally, I have had to call students to my office and have a private conference about friends visiting in person or cell phone use, but I would never approach them in front of their friends. I keep it on a professional level. If the problems persist, after a couple of counseling sessions they are not rehired.

Conni: Getting students to work the "undesirable hours" was my biggest challenge. To overcome it, I discussed the hours in the application interview so that potential student assistants were aware up front that they would be expected to work those hours. I also set up a rotating schedule so that no two students (two worked each hour) had to bear the burden alone. Students were also responsible for finding a replacement if they could not work.

(Cont'd.)

Managers' Roundtable Discussion *(Continued)*

Michael: I'm relatively new in my position, and when I came in, the students were heavily controlled by the interim supervisor. It has been challenging to assert my leadership over the situation and get students to recognize that they have a new boss.

Gary: The biggest challenge for me is creating a schedule. At Sarah Lawrence College (SLC) schedules change for many students every semester. Due to this, large amounts of time are spent on the creation of the fall and spring schedules for three spaces—PC/Mac Lab, Mac Lab, and the ACD Office. We have not come to a definitive solution yet. Something that has appeared to help is the scheduling of large blocks of hours versus small blocks. A student that works 4 hours is more likely to work their shift than someone scheduled for only 2 hours. Class schedules do not always accommodate this type of scheduling so I/we are forced to offer short shifts to fill in the gaps. One additional topic that causes frustration and confusion around campus is wage. SLC does not have a standard wage in place for student employees. Therefore, a student may make one wage for one job and another for a similar job.

Nick: The biggest challenge is interviewing, hiring, scheduling, and training the students at the beginning of the school year, all within a short time frame. I overcome this by being organized and well prepared ahead of time. I try to re-hire students who worked for us the previous year and during the hiring process I try to hire students who are likely to return the following year. This way, I minimize the number of new hires each September. This eases the pressure, especially on interviewing and training, which can be both time-consuming and difficult to schedule while trying to balance my other duties during the busy month of September.

Scott Hanscom, Johns Hopkins University
Werner Haun, Library of Congress
Bonnie Hines, Louisiana State University of Alexandria
Conni Kitten, Texas Tech University Libraries

Michael Miller, Queens College—City University
  of New York
Gary Ploski, Sarah Lawrence College
Nick Rizzo, University of British Columbia

---

to be sure that staff could adjust to the new procedures. Once the workflow was streamlined, Martin and her colleagues looked at staffing to determine if, under new and more efficient procedures, current staffing was appropriate. Although McMaster University's primary purpose was not to determine the need for student assistants, their process for examining workflow could be used for that purpose.

REDESIGN INEFFICIENT WORKFLOW PROCEDURES

> "Redesign usually involves simplifying the work process by eliminating non value-added activities, reintegrating the remaining steps and, if necessary, using automation as the means to bring the redesign about."
> —Robert Lukas, "A Skeptic Tries It and Likes It," 1992

Once you have created workflow process maps and completed job audits, take a look at how current practices are working for your department. There may be tasks or workflows that can be streamlined or perhaps even eliminated. Is everyone being used to their fullest potential? Do upper-level staff have enough time to perform the tasks and functions that they alone can do, or is their time bogged down by tasks that someone else, perhaps a student, could do? Try to think creatively, and try not to get distracted by sacred cows—those practices that we hold on to because we have always held on to them. There are no sacred cows in the workflow audit, and by continually asking yourself, "Why do we do it that way?" and "How could we do that more efficiently?" you will be able to think creatively about change. Some departments have determined that students can perform tasks that were previously done only by librarians, while others have given tasks formerly assigned to staff to supervisors.

To determine if you need student assistance, take a look at the workflow you are considering adding a student worker to perform. What isn't working? What could work better? What are you hoping to accomplish? What tasks are you considering a student for? Why is a student an appropriate choice? Could the same results be accomplished by re-engineering the workflow?

By examining what staff are doing during their entire workday and analyzing every task they perform, you are likely to identify low payoff or no-payoff tasks that can be eliminated. You may also identify tasks they are not doing that they should be doing (Lukas, 1992: 27). Looking at all of this information will help you to gain a better idea of how the department does what it does, and how it could be done more efficiently. With a few minor adjustments additional people may not be necessary. As you examine tasks, reshuffling as necessary, you should also become aware if you need additional people to take on some of the work and what level of staff those new hires need to be at. Often, when a need for additional staff is identified the first staff hired are student assistants. The workflow audit will identify some possible task reconfigurations.

USING WORKFLOW TASKS TO DESIGN AN EFFECTIVE JOB DESCRIPTION

When thinking about jobs that are appropriate for students, think about how you and your organization would feel about potential job responsibilities, such as money handling or students working with little or no supervision being assigned, and to what degree students should assist patrons. While students themselves are not likely to be represented by a union, other unions on campus may take issue with certain tasks being assigned to student assistants. Don't make any staffing decisions in a vacuum, but rather discuss your

My student assistants seem bored by their assignments. What should I do?

Remind them of the context of what they do, and how important it is to the mission and services of the library. For example, shelf reading is a daunting task, but if you tell students that a book mis-shelved is as good as lost, and show them the statistical evidence that indicates that increased shelf reading makes the library easier to use, they will understand the importance of the job. If it will not interfere with patron service or quality work, consider allowing students to use their iPods during more routine tasks.

Prepare all staff for change by telling them about it early and often.

ideas with your supervisor and/or human resources department throughout the process. When considering the tasks that may comprise a student job, consider the skills needed for the job. For instance, if independent judgment is required, an upper-division undergraduate or graduate student might be the most appropriate choice. Special skills are also important to identify at this early stage, such as foreign language or specific technical proficiency. Think about the times of year that will be most busy for this position, and if it would be advisable to hire a student who lives locally or has a certain major with an unusual time frame for work demands so that he or she would be available to work during busy times. How many hours per week would you like someone to work? Will this position act as a back-up for full-time staff?

Frequently, examining the tasks performed in a department leads to hiring student workers to perform essential or time-specific tasks. If this is the case, it is advisable to devise a contingency plan for absences. Chapters 6 and 7 of this book will provide you with strategies for keeping absences to a minimum, but you must have a plan in place in case you are faced with an absence. The planning stages are as good a time as any to determine your options. Particularly if retention has been an issue, you may wish to consider building a student "job ladder" into you department. In a job ladder, you have incrementally more difficult (and better-paying) student jobs, so you can build in promotions. Job ladders are more fully explored in chapter 7.

Once you have audited your department's workflow you will begin to see where the gaps in coverage lie. Think about who does what and how appropriate current assignments are. Is a high-level staff member labeling books? Perhaps this person's time could be better spent. Think about how tasks can be better divided so that everyone has a reasonable amount of work to do. As you reassign tasks you will see that several tasks remain unassigned (or under-assigned). These are the tasks to assign to student assistants.

MATCH TASKS TO COMPETENCIES

What could student assistants do? What tasks, steps, projects need to be assigned to someone? Would anyone on staff be an appropriate choice for these tasks? Make a laundry list of the tasks that need attention. Do any of them logically group together? Are any of them appropriate for student workers, such as to

- assist with book searches;
- maintain hold shelf (keep books in proper order, remove expired holds, search stacks for missing holds);
- staff exit (check bags if alarm sounds, examine library books to ensure they are charged out);
- mail notices (print notices, fold notices, stuff envelopes);
- check in materials, particularly during busy times?

As things in the department change, people may feel threatened and they may not think additional help is necessary. The way to address this is by applying some change management strategies. When anticipating a change, be sure to provide as much information as possible. As Cheryl Martin's successful experience with workflow redesign indicates, getting staff involved in the change helps them to overcome any initial mistrust they may experience. Make a clear case for hiring additional students by first clearly articulating what the students' roles will be and how they may effect the role of established staff.

Why do people resist change? Fear, loss of control? Don't see the need for the change? There are five basic reasons why people resist change, and knowing them can help you to minimize the resistance (Maxwell, 1992: 48–49).

1. Economic—people fear they will lose their jobs
2. Political—people feel vulnerable facing the unknown
3. Inconvenience—people would rather continue functioning in the status quo than be bothered learning something new
4. Loss of control—people are reluctant to give up their feeling of mastery over their jobs, even temporarily
5. Lack of information—people do not have enough information to understand what the changes are and why they are being made.

Whatever the reason, it's natural for people to resist change. Resistance may manifest itself in any one of a number of different ways. People may ignore the impending change and hope it goes away; they may exhibit signs of anger; they may talk badly or spread false rumors about the change. By helping staff to be prepared for the change, you can minimize their discomfort.

Early on (before the change)

1. Carefully and tactfully describe the change and why it is needed
2. Discuss possible effects and outcomes
3. Ask for reactions, allowing time for people to think about it
4. Allow for a continuing conversation
5. Talk about new skills that will be beneficial during and after the change
6. Encourage constructive communication in all directions
7. Clear up any misunderstandings
8. Solicit ideas for improvement

During the Change

1. Discuss people's needs (patience, additional training, etc.)
2. Stress that change is a process, and that everyone will get through it
3. Develop contingency plans, soliciting input from everyone involved

After the Change

1. Reinforce that it is a process, and there might be issues to improve for some time
2. Engage everyone involved in problem solving
3. Communicate, Communicate, Communicate
4. Commit to continuous improvement

Figure 2-2. Managing Change

There is a tremendous amount of turnover in our student worker jobs. How can I increase retention?

Take a look at what you are asking students to do, and how you are asking. If you are asking them to do something that seems deathly boring, but really needs to get done, be sure to explain the context of why the task is important. If students know that what they are doing matters, they are more likely to own the task.

Perhaps a student could stuff envelopes while he or she is staffing the exit? Perhaps a student could assist with various types of stack searching, such as looking for holds that mistakenly were reshelved as well as items that patrons believe they have returned. Maybe they could even pull interlibrary loan books or books to be processed for reserve while they are in the stacks. The tasks you group together should not be too various. Student jobs are generally more successful with a fairly limited scope. For example, it might be too much for a student to be responsible for processing books for course reserve and labeling new acquisitions. Hopefully, the tasks you identify will group nicely into one or more job description, and each grouping will be of a manageable scope for one person to master in a 10–15-hour work week. Write a working draft of the job description, but be prepared to be flexible since funding has not yet been secured. Examples of job descriptions are shown in figure 2-3.

Job Title:	Exit Assistant
Competencies:	• attention to detail • good customer service attitude • tolerance for stress
Tasks (including percentages):	• ensure security of library materials. Monitor exit, and when alarm sounds, inspect patron's bags (65%) • assist patrons by answering directional questions and referring patrons to appropriate departments when necessary (20%) • assist circulation desk by printing and mailing monthly statements and invoices (15%)
Special Physical Requirements:	
Wage:	$6.75/hour
Job Title:	Stacks Assistant
Competencies:	• ability to follow directions • good personal organization • attention to detail
Tasks (including percentages):	• accurately shelve library materials (60%) • assist with searches (e.g., for holds, delivery service, ILL, Reserve processing, etc.) (40%)
Special Physical Requirements:	• ability to push a book cart (approximately 40 pounds)
Wage:	$6.75/hour

Figure 2-3. Job Description Examples

Job Title:	Copy Cataloging Assistant
Competencies:	• knowledge of at least one non-Roman language • attention to detail
Tasks (including percentages):	• search bibliographic utilities for cataloging copy (40%) • assist with catalog editing and maintenance (edit and merge records, add copies, transfer locations, withdraw missing items) (30%) • label materials, physically transfer materials to other locations (25%)
Special Physical Requirements:	• ability to push a book cart (approx. 40 pounds) • ability to work in a dusty environment
Wage:	$8.00 hour

Figure 2-3. Job Description Examples *(Continued)*

Once you have determined the tasks and responsibilities that will comprise the job, it will be fairly straightforward to identify the knowledge, skills, and abilities necessary to carry out successfully those tasks and responsibilities. The skills and abilities necessary to be successful at a job are known as job competencies. Figure 2-4 illustrates job tasks and the competencies that relate to them.

Identify the competencies needed to be successful at a job early on in the job design process, as they will inform the job description, help to determine the wage paid, be valuable during the interview process, and be helpful as you prepare training materials. Job competencies are also essential during the interview process to determine if potential candidates possess the necessary competencies.

Task	Competency(ies)
Circulation Desk (check in, check out)	• attention to detail • tolerance for stress • customer service attitude
Labeling	• attention to detail • good manual dexterity
Serials check in	• attention to detail • foreign language transliteration skills
Copy cataloging	• reading knowledge of one or more foreign language • attention to detail

Figure 2-4. Tasks and Related Competencies

> To identify job competencies, think of someone who has had success in a job similar to the one you wish to fill. What was it about that person that made him her her successful? (Padilla and Patterson, 1992: 6).

WRITE A SUCCESSFUL JOB DESCRIPTION

Once you have determined the tasks that will comprise the job, and the specific competencies necessary to be successful at those tasks, you have all of the information you need to write a job description. The job description should be clear and concise, and should allow for some degree of flexibility. It serves as the background documentation for the job ad, the training materials, and, ultimately, the key to evaluating the success of the people you hire for the position, but first and foremost it is part of the documentation you need in order to get the job approved. Along with the job audit (which could make an argument for additional student staff) and the workflow audit (which shows that you have explored other options), the job description will be necessary for your boss and/or human resources department to review to determine (1) if the job will be approved and (2) if it is approved, what the pay scale will be.

> **I can't get my boss to approve funding for much-needed student assistant positions—Help!**
>
> Be sure to make a convincing case for your need. Include the data that shows that you need one or more additional positions (e.g., we can label x books per hour, and we currently employ students for y hours; therefore, we need to increase our student workforce by x/y). Workflow audit data from the worksheets you complete at the end of chapter 2 will also help to solidify your argument.

REQUEST APPROVAL

Obtain an overview of the rules governing Federal Work Study, along with the local student employee rules and procedures at your institution. Most likely you will need to get approval for a new student assistant position. The information you collected in your workflow audit should provide you with ample evidence to support the creation of a student position and the number of students who should be hired.

FITTING DEPARTMENTAL NEEDS WITH CAMPUS REGULATIONS

Just as it is essential to know your departmental needs, it's vital to know your campus regulations when it comes to hiring student workers. Talk to your library or campus human resources representatives, or whomever has oversight for student worker issues.

SECURE AMPLE FUNDING

Your careful consideration of the tasks the student(s) will perform will also provide your human resources staff with enough information to advise you on the pay scale for the job. Generally, students will be paid the library's basic pay rate unless the job requires (Russell, 1995: 100):

1. Night hours
2. Previous off-campus experience
3. Supervisory responsibility
4. Graduate student maturity
5. Previous library experience

With your job description and an understanding of the factors that influence pay rate, you can approach whomever it is at your library who can authorize a new student budget or an increase to your student budget line. Once you know the appropriate pay scale for the job and have an idea of how many hours per week of student labor you'd like to hire for, you can easily calculate how much money you will need to fund the position. This calculation gets a little tricky when attempting to predict whether the percentage of students you wish to hire will have a work study allotment. However, you can certainly ask your human resources officer or financial aid department the overall percentage of students who receive a federal work study award, and use that as an estimate. For example, if, at your college or university, 20 percent of students receive work study you can estimate that 20 percent of the students you hire will have a work study award. Multiply the percentage of student staff that have a work study award by the percentage of wages that your department is responsible for paying and add that to the wages that you will have to pay to employ any non-work study students in your department.

Have all of your documentation (job audit, workflow analysis, defined competencies, job description, pay scale information from the human resources department) in a presentable, clear, concise form for your boss, or whomever makes the decision to increase your student budget for your new position(s). Even in flush times, funding is a touchy subject, and administrators are not keen to fund a new budget line without a specific, documented need. So, be sure to do your homework, and be sure to show the person making the funding decisions that you have done your homework.

> Use data gathered during the job design process to convince senior administrators that a new or additional student position is necessary.

---

1. Identify the Need
2. Streamline Workflows
3. Design the Job
4. Get Approval for the Job
5. Secure Funding

Figure 2-5. Five Steps before You Recruit

CONCLUSION

Before you hire, make sure you really need to hire by auditing workflows and job assignments of current staff. Simple changes to existing workflows may obviate the need for student help. If you do determine that you need to hire additional staff, the workflow analysis you conduct will be the data required to back up your request for funding. Thorough preparation ensures that you really need to hire additional staff. It also ensures that any jobs you do create will be well thought out and easy to fill.

EXERCISES

EXERCISE 2-1: JOB AUDIT WORKSHEET (TO BE COMPLETED BY ALL STAFF)

Instructions: Please log your time for one week. We are examining our workflows and trying to determine ways to work more efficiently. It is important that you be as accurate as possible.

Time	Task

Are there any projects you are interested in taking on or learning?

Are there any of your current projects that you'd like to pass along to someone else?

What are your suggestions about ways we could do things better, faster or more efficiently?

EXERCISE 2-2: WORKFLOW AUDIT SIMPLIFIED

List the workflows in your department

1. _____ 4. _____
2. _____ 5. _____
3. _____ 6. _____

List all of the steps involved in each workflow

1. _____ 4. _____
    a. _____   a. _____
    b. _____   b. _____
    c. _____   c. _____
    d. _____   d. _____
    e. _____   e. _____

2. _____ 5. _____
    a. _____   a. _____
    b. _____   b. _____
    c. _____   c. _____
    d. _____   d. _____
    e. _____   e. _____

3. _____ 6. _____
    a. _____   a. _____
    b. _____   b. _____
    c. _____   c. _____
    d. _____   d. _____
    e. _____   e. _____

Answer the following questions:

What isn't working?	
Who does what (the "who" can be the job title, especially if more than one person carries out the task, or the actual person)?	
What is the reason for each step?	
What could we simply stop doing?	
If we stopped doing X, what would we need to do to prepare?	
What could be done better? How?	
How can automation help us?	
Who has time in their day to take care of (some or all of) this (job audit)?	

List your options (without judging them)

A. _____

B. _____

C. _____

D. _____

E. _____

Judge your options

EXERCISE 2-3: QUESTIONS TO ASK YOUR HUMAN RESOURCES DEPARTMENT

1. How does student hiring usually work?

2. What is the approval process for job descriptions?

3. How much control do I have over who is hired?

4. Can I hire independently? (If not, how can I increase the chances that whoever is doing the hiring will best meet your needs?)

5. What is my departmental budget for student assistants? How would I go about requesting an increase if necessary?

6. What are the regulations regarding work study?

7. Are there salary scales for student workers? What are they?

8. Must I hire work study students? (If yes, ask why.)

9. How much can I pay?

10. Am I allowed to hire international students? If yes, ask about specific regulations or procedures you'll need to know about.

11. Can I hire students from other campuses or local, non-affiliated colleges or universities? (If yes, ask about any specific regulations or procedures you should know about.)

12. How many hours can a student work in a given week? How does this fluctuate during school vacations?

13. Are there any local specific regulations about student employment of which I should be aware? (e.g., restrictions on first-year students working, minimum required GPA, etc.)

14. Can I increase student responsibilities without creating problems with the union?

15. Are students allowed to supervise other students?

16. Are there any other institutional policies or procedures I should know about?

REFERENCES

"The Deming System of Profound Knowledge." The W. Edwards Deming Institute. September 19, 2005. www.deming.org/theman/teaching.html and www.deming.org/theman/teachings2.html.

Giesecke, Joan. "Performance appraisal." *In Practical Help for New Supervisors*. Edited by Joan Giesecke. Chicago: American Library Association, 1992.

Hayes, Jan, and Maureen Sullivan. "Mapping the Process: Engaging Staff in Work Redesign." *Library Administration and Management* 17, 2 (Spring 2003): 87–93.

Jerabek, Ann. "Job Descriptions: Don't Hire Without Them." *Journal of Interlibrary Loan, Document Delivery and Information Supply* 13, 3 (2003): 113–126.

Lin, Yei Fang, and Brian H. Kleiner. "How to Hire Employees Effectively." *Management Research News* 27, 4/5 (2004): 108–115.

Lukas, Robert R. "A Skeptic Tries It and Likes It." *Inform* 5 (1992): 27.

Martin, Cheryl. "Workflow Analysis as a Basis for Organizational Redesign at McMaster University Library." In *Innovative Redesign and Reorganization of Library Technical Services: Paths for the Future and Case Studies*. Edited by Bradford Lee Eden. Westport, CT: Libraries Unlimited, 2004.

Maxwell, Jan. "Managing Change." In *Practical Help for New Supervisors*. Edited by Joan Giesecke. Chicago. American Library Association, 1992.

Nelson, Bob, and Peter Economy. *Managing for Dummies*. Foster City, CA: IDG Books, 1996.

Rimmer, Anne. "Interviewing." In *Practical Help for New Supervisors*. Edited by Joan Gieseke. Chicago: American Library Association, 1992.

Russell, Thyra K. "Student Employmennt Manuals." *Journal of Library Administration* 21, 3/4 (1995): 95–108.

Sullivan, Maureen. "Reflections on Academic Libraries as Self-Organizing Systems: Ways Leaders Can Support Staff." *ACRL News* 60, 5 (May 1999): 393–394.

Turner, Anne M. "Making Personnel Studies Work." *Library Journal* 28, (2003): 54.

3 SIMPLIFYING THE HIRING PROCESS

WHY DEVELOP A HIRING FRAMEWORK?

How do I know what to include in a job description?

Include the core tasks that you will be asking the student to perform. Think about why you want to hire a student, and what you want that person to do, and include those items.

As a supervisor of library student assistants, there really is no way to get around the recruitment process. Even with very low turnover among your student workers, you will probably still have to recruit annually. Rather than think of this as a daunting process to start from scratch each year, create a framework that can be recycled year after year. This framework, called a vacancy toolkit, includes your prepared job descriptions, job advertisements, interview questions, reference checking questions, and everything else you need to get you through the hiring process. By outlining and preparing the hiring process one time, you reduce the time spent on hiring to actual hiring efforts each year, rather than preparing those efforts.

OUTLINING AN ACCURATE JOB DESCRIPTION

Written job descriptions are essential for all positions, including student assistant positions. Even if job descriptions are not required by your institution, they will be extremely valuable to you and to the students you hire for the job. These written descriptions outline what students will be doing, and will assist you in writing interview questions, selecting candidates, training new hires, and evaluating job performance. Job descriptions should include the fundamental elements of the job, or, in other words, what you need done. They should also be explicit about the education level the job demands, and the pay scale of the job. Job descriptions are internal documents that help you and the employee to have an understanding of what the job involves, and are not to be confused with the job ad, which is used for recruiting purposes.

All jobs—even student jobs—
must have a written job
description.

How do you get started writing a student worker job description? If you
have any experience writing job descriptions for other staff, you know the
process. Your first step is to check in with your human resources department, or perhaps your supervisor, to see if a template for student worker
job descriptions has already been developed at your library or college. If
not, see the generic template at the end of this chapter. If you have been
following the steps in this manual, you have already identified the basic information that you need for your new job description by identifying job
competencies, essential tasks, and workflows. The job description is simply
an organized format in which to present this information. To review:

- Competency—an essential skill needed to be successful
  in the job
- Essential Task—a core component of a job
- Workflow—how something is done, including all steps
  involved.

You already have an idea of both the job competencies related to the
job you are describing and the tasks involved, since you identified them
through the exercises in chapter 1 (see also Figure 2.3). Job descriptions
should include specific, measurable tasks that the student will be responsible for carrying out. Student assistant job descriptions do not differ significantly in content from regular staff and professional job descriptions, but
may differ in format, as prescribed by your institution. They should include
the tasks and responsibilities the student will be responsible for as well as
a brief description of the competencies identified for the job and any special physical requirements (ability to push a book cart of approximately

If you have never written a job description before, the task may seem
daunting. Don't worry, just think about the various aspects of the job. If
you were to make a pie chart of the job, which functions would be the
"slices" of pie? List each component of the job. If someone is already
working in the job, ask them what they spend their time on, or shadow
them for a few days. The job description exists to keep you and the staff
member performing the job on the same page as far as the duties that
will be expected of him or her. Make sure the job description includes a
list of all the duties the incumbent is expected to carry out, and the
percentage of the person's workweek that should be spent on each task.

Keep subjective phrases and ambiguity out of the job description. Each
task should be a bullet point in the description, followed by a clear,
concise description of what the task involves. One of the best ways to
write a job description is by modeling it on existing job descriptions, so
ask your colleagues for samples before you begin writing.

Figure 3-1. How to Write Job Descriptions

```
1.  Obtain approval to rehire
2.  Post the advertisement
3.  Review resumes
4.  Set aside time to interview
5.  E-mail/call top candidates to set up interview
6.  Conduct interviews
7.  Check references
8.  Make offer(s) and get paperwork requirements completed
9.  Set schedule
10. Get passwords/accounts, etc.
```

Figure 3-2. Steps to Take When You Have a Vacancy

40 pounds) and/or environmental conditions (high tolerance for a dusty workplace).

ASSEMBLING THE COMPONENTS OF A VACANCY TOOLKIT

The purpose of the vacancy toolkit is to make the hiring process as easy as possible and to keep you from having to reinvent the hiring process each and every time you have a vacancy. The vacancy toolkit consists of all forms, electronic documents, and reminders you need to hire someone new, including any human resources paperwork, the job ad, job description, interview questions, job competencies, reference checking worksheets, and any other paperwork needed. Having these documents prepared and well organized will allow you to post the job the moment you determine a need without wasting valuable time gathering the tools necessary to fill a vacancy.

Having a vacancy toolkit is a foolproof way to get students hired without expending unnecessary intellectual energy on the process. The vacancy toolkit consists of the following ten parts:

1. The Hiring Check List
2. The Job Ad
3. Telephone Script for Setting Up Interviews
4. Interview Questions
5. Job Description

I just dread turnover because every time I have to hire a new student the process is so much work. How can I make it a little easier?

Spend a little time setting up your vacancy toolkit. Make sure it has everything you need to use to hire, so that you don't need to start from scratch each time you have a vacancy. Having a well planned vacancy toolkit will save you a lot of work in the long run.

Managers' Roundtable Discussion

Question: How do you make the hiring process easy on yourself?

Scott: I use a checklist to make sure I've covered all the bases (e.g., workstudy, I-9 form, availability, etc.).

Werner: I believe the hiring process is easier if you follow a set format and list of questions. This ensures you gather necessary information to compare applicants fairly and accurately.

Bonnie: We work at a small school, so I ask faculty, staff, or the financial aid office for recommendations. I've also received good recommendations from our best student workers. I would never hire "cold" and always have some background on potential new hires.

Conni: Set up an excellent interview template. (Our library has a student assistant job posting template; I kept mine filled out and on my desktop.) When I needed to hire a student, I e-mailed it to Personnel and asked them to post the position.

Michael: The hiring process is centralized on our campus, so I have very little control over it, and therefore very little work to do regarding screening resumes or interviewing potential student assistants. Training is another story, because we are trying to improve the caliber of student assistant we hire. I share training responsibilities with department staff.

Gary: I make the process easier by inviting good students to work with us again and recruiting friends of present or past employees. Both strategies have yielded fantastic results.

Nick: I make the hiring process easier by preparing and organizing ahead of time. I normally create a schedule that works for the library and its needs, and then try to hire good students whose own schedules mesh with it. However, there is some flexibility. I will try to accommodate students who have worked for us before and are good workers. I also prepare interview questions and tests ahead of time. I try to re-hire as many good previous student workers as possible. This makes for less time spent interviewing and training new students.

Question: How do you keep students from "flaking out" at the end of the semester?

Scott: I don't prevent students from flaking out, I expect that they will. The students here truly are assistants in the department, so the regular staff know that while the students are here to help us, we are ultimately responsible for getting the work done, with or without student assistants.

Werner: I deal with the unavoidable end-of-semester unreliability by remaining as flexible as possible. Typically, preservation work is less time sensitive than the work in other parts of the library, which has enabled me to more easily adjust their schedule. In this way, they might be better able to fit in some hours rather than not working at all. This flexibility can also go a long way in creating good will between a supervisor and a student worker, whereby when their schedule allows they will be more willing to accommodate the needs of your department.

Bonnie: I develop an "end-of-the-semester schedule" that allows for more flexibility. Students who can work during exams are given extra hours so those who can't don't have to. Once the "end-of-semester-schedule" is agreed upon, students understand that if they don't work this schedule, they will not be re-hired at the beginning of the next semester.

Conni: Preventing unreliability is a challenge at the end of the semester because students are tired by that point. You have to remind them that they're here to do a job and that's what we and our patrons expect. Also it doesn't hurt to show them extra appreciation and to give them "goody bags" full of candy, cookies, soft drinks, etc., for finals.

(Cont'd.)

Managers' Roundtable Discussion *(Continued)*

Michael: I allow students to work hours other than what they usually do, including shorter shifts and different blocks of time. Generally, I create a different "finals week" schedule where students sign up for the hours they can work.

Gary: I have conversations with student workers as often as possible. The simplest conversation about a book they've been reading, a class they've just finished, or other topics of interest. This type of interaction seems to provide an opportunity for a student to say how difficult things are or how great things are with their class(es). Also, it gives them a chance to see that I/we are not uncaring people without any intention to listen to their troubles.

Nick: I try to be flexible. If students need to have a day off or need to switch shifts because they have exams or papers due, I try to accommodate them. I tell them if they can't work a shift, to let me know ahead of time so that we can work something out. I usually have another student who is willing to switch a shift or work extra hours if someone else can't. Having been a student myself, I realize that their studies are their first priority, so I try to meet them halfway.

Scott Hanscom, Johns Hopkins University
Werner Haun, Library of Congress
Bonnie Hines, Louisiana State University of Alexandria
Conni Kitten, Texas Tech University Libraries

Michael Miller, Queens College—City University of New York
Gary Ploski, Sarah Lawrence College
Nick Rizzo, University of British Columbia

---

6. Reference Check Worksheet
7. Offer Telephone Script
8. Schedule Guidelines
9. Contact Information
10. Passwords and Security Needs

> Keep all parts of the vacancy toolkit as one file so you have everything together when it's time to hire.

THE HIRING CHECKLIST

The hiring checklist incorporates every step you need to take to get a student assistant hired. As a reminder of various steps you need to take and forms you need to complete, it should include items such as "obtain approval to hire," "send job ad to HR," and "New Hires fill out I9 and W4 forms." It's a great tool to keep you on track with the hiring procedure and ensure that the process goes smoothly.

THE JOB AD

In particular, if turnover is high in your department, you'll want the job ad prepared so that you can begin the process at a moment's notice. The beginning of the semester is a busy time of year. Reserve materials need to

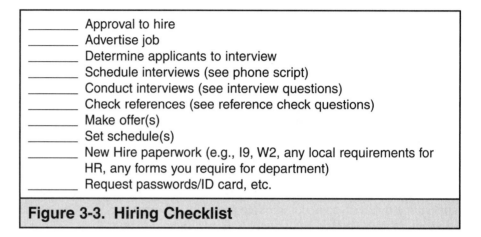

_____ Approval to hire
_____ Advertise job
_____ Determine applicants to interview
_____ Schedule interviews (see phone script)
_____ Conduct interviews (see interview questions)
_____ Check references (see reference check questions)
_____ Make offer(s)
_____ Set schedule(s)
_____ New Hire paperwork (e.g., I9, W2, any local requirements for HR, any forms you require for department)
_____ Request passwords/ID card, etc.

Figure 3-3. Hiring Checklist

be processed and posted, students need directions around the library, staff is stretched thin providing orientation classes and tours for new students. By having a job ad ready, you can save time and energy in the recruitment process, particularly at crucial times of the year. The job ad should be free of jargon and represent the job in the best possible light. The ad is your primary recruitment tool, so make sure it will attract the type of applicant you are looking for.

THE TELEPHONE SCRIPT FOR SETTING UP INTERVIEWS

Having a telephone script makes it absolutely foolproof to set up interviews with prospective student workers. With a written script, you have no excuse for putting off making telephone calls to set up interviews, since little or no intellectual effort will be required. It also makes it possible to delegate the task of setting up interviews to a staff member or currently employed student worker.

Looking for an interesting job to help you learn your way around the library? We'll train you to use various databases and tools to help us lend items in our collection to libraries across the country and around the world. If you have a good eye for detail, enjoy following clues to track down information, can push a book cart weighing 40 pounds and don't mind picking up the occasional dusty book, please e-mail Joe at joe.smith@college.edu, attaching your resume, the days and times you are able to work, the number of hours you'd like to work per week, and the names and phone numbers of 3 people who can serve as a reference for you. $6.50/hour, college work study preferred (but not required).

Figure 3-4. The Job Ad

May I speak to _____
This is Joe from the Interlibrary Loan office at the Frasier Library at Blah Blah College.

I received your application for our lending assistant position, and I'd like to set up an appointment with you.

Before I do, though, I want to tell you a little bit about the job. We need to hire some people to help us out lending materials to other libraries. The students who currently work in the department like it because it's kind of like going on a scavenger hunt or being a detective. We provide you with the information you need to find the book or article, then you track it down. They also like it because it helps them to know how to use the library. I should mention that it's a really busy department, and never a dull job. But, it's not the kind of work study job where you can do your homework at work. Does that sound like something you'd be interested in?

I have the following dates/times available

Figure 3-5. Phone Script for Setting Up Interviews

THE INTERVIEW QUESTIONS

Interview questions should address the main competencies required in the job. As opposed to asking abstract questions, asking questions about an applicant's experience with various skills that they'll need for the job is more predictive of future performance. Each applicant should be asked the same questions, as that keeps the interview process fair and helps you to compare the applicants you interview to one another more easily. Using prepared questions also means that interview questions can be written in advance and that, once you spend time writing questions, you'll be able to re-use them year after year with only minor revisions to keep them fresh.

THE JOB DESCRIPTION

Job descriptions clearly outline the fundamental elements of the job. Without a written job description to which both supervisor and student have access, it is almost impossible to be sure both parties have a shared understanding of what the job involves. The job description needs to be on hand to provide to applicants you are interviewing, as it will help you to articulate clearly job requirements (Slagell and Langendorfer, 2003: 280). It is also essential for ongoing evaluation of the employee, and the employee needs a copy so he or she will have a written record of the job requirements (Gieseke, 1992: 21).

Print one sheet for each interviewee

Name:

Date of Interview:

— Welcome to Blah Blah college
— When did you arrive?

a. Opening Small Talk
   — Welcome to XXX College
   — When did you arrive on campus?
   — Did you have any trouble finding the office?

b. Tell me about a time when you had to pay really close attention to something to get it right.

c. Tell me about an experience you had in which you had to deal with deadlines.

d. Tell me about an experience you had learning something completely new.

Figure 3-6. Interview Questions

Job Title:	ILL Assistant
Competencies:	• Attention to detail
Tasks (including percentages):	• search RLG, OCLC and find requested material (50%)
	• post articles to Web (40%)
	• process books borrowed from other libraries (20%)
Special Physical Requirements:	• ability to push a book cart (approx. 40 pounds)
	• ability to use a computer and mouse
Wage:	$7.50/hour

Figure 3-7. Job Description

THE REFERENCE CHECK WORKSHEET

Checking references is one of the most valuable tools in the selection process. Nowhere else can you get honest feedback about the actual past performance of the applicants. Interview questions will help you to assess the candidate's potential for the actual tasks involved in the job, but the references will give you information on the general behavioral characteristics that must be at a certain standard for the candidate to be successful. No other part of the selection process will tell you about the applicant's punctuality, attendance, and objective comments on the quality of his or her job performance. Using a prepared worksheet makes it easy to keep a written record of the information that each reference provides.

THE OFFER SCRIPT

Making a job offer can be awkward, but planning it out in advance can help to make it less difficult. If you know where the conversation is going, it will be a more comfortable experience for both you and the person to whom you are offering the job. Unlike the phone script for setting up interviews, it is not advisable to delegate this step of the process. Wage information, an essential part of the offer, should be kept confidential. But, planning out the script will make it easier for you to extend offers, even if you are completely exhausted from the hiring process.

THE SCHEDULING GUIDELINES

While scheduling needs may not remain constant for each hiring cycle, it's important to keep this step in the process so that you don't forget to establish mutually agreed upon work schedules with your new hires. This conversation should take place after the offer is accepted. When negotiating a schedule with a new hire, articulate the length of time they will be held to the agreed upon schedule. Is it until exam week or for the entire semester? Are they obligated to work on holidays and school vacations? What happens if on a given Tuesday, the college holds Monday classes? What happens in cases of inclement weather? What if the student is ill? What if he or she realizes they are over committed? All of these issues should be discussed prior to the student's first day of work, then reiterated during the training process.

Hi, _____. This is Joe from Frasier Library. How are you? I'm calling to offer you the job as Interlibrary Loan Assistant, at $7.50 per hour. Are you interested? Great. We'd like you to work Monday, Tuesday and Wednesday from 9 to 12—are you still able to do that? Great. Can you start on Monday?

Figure 3-8. Offer Script (including schedule conversation and invitation to stop by to fill out paperwork)

	M	T	W	T	F
9–10					
10–11					
11–12					
12–1					
1–2					
2–3					
3–4					
4–5					
5–6					

Figure 3-9. Schedule Setting

CONTACT INFORMATION

In the event of an emergency, a staffing shortage, or an unexcused absence, you may need to get in touch with one or more students. Use the post-offer conversation to obtain contact information—mobile phone number, e-mail, local address, and home address—so that you will be able to get in touch with your new hire.

Name	
E-mail	
Phone	
Local Address	
Home Address (where you would like your final check mailed)	
Emergency Contact	

Figure 3-10. Contact Information

Windows Network
    Requested:
    Received:

Circulation System
    Requested:
    Received:

ILL Manager
    Created:

Figure 3-11. Password Tickler

PASSWORDS AND SECURITY NEEDS

Your new hire will most likely need at least one computer password. If you are not the person to actually create the password(s), you'll need to request what is required from the appropriate people. If you have hired someone who is not a student at your institution (perhaps he or she is a high school student or a student at another local college or university) or if you work in a public library and are hiring students, you may need to obtain an identification card for the new hire. You may assign lockers to your student workers. All passwords and security issues should be detailed in your new hire toolkit.

SCHEDULING

Keep in mind the staffing needs of the department at the early hiring stages. Students should commit to a set schedule at the point of hire, with the understanding that if it becomes too much, you will adjust their schedules as needed. After all, while accommodating every scheduling need of every student can become burdensome, you'd rather reduce someone's hours than have them quit altogether. Before you hire, you should determine what times of the day and days of the week you need people to work, and how many people you need per each time slot. Think about your need on evenings and weekends, especially if new hires will be working unsupervised, and what level of maturity you are looking for to fill those spots.

    Set the schedule with students at the point of hire. It is far too time-consuming for you, and confusing for student workers, to determine a different schedule each week. Try to strike a balance between being too rigid and letting students run roughshod over you and the schedule. There are

Student workers tend to stop coming to work around finals time, and scheduling gets really disorganized. What can I do to prevent this?

Keep in mind that a student's world revolves around the academic year. Make one set schedule that runs for the length of the semester, one for each vacation or holiday, one for the reading period, and another for finals. In addition to emphasizing that you need people to work during those times, it will allow those students who wish to pick up extra hours the opportunity to do so, and those who need to study or who will otherwise not be available for work will be more reliable during the "regular" semester.

many options for managing a student schedule. One way to do this is to inform students up front that they are expected to come to work unless they are ill, and that calling in sick when they are not ill is a serious infraction that will result in termination. Another way to do this is to require students to arrange their own substitute if they are unable to work an assigned shift. Think about the procedures that will work best for you and the department.

> The amount of training given is an inverse proportion to the number of hours a student works. That is, the fewer hours a student is exposed to a job, the more training he or she will need.

It is only fair to students, and provides the best results, if you set up different schedules for different points in the school year, that is to say, have one schedule for the majority of the semester, then switch to the finals schedule when classes end. There are just as many students who are willing to work additional shifts during finals week as there are students who do not elect to work, so you and the department will be covered without the hassle of students who can't work because they need to study, finish a paper, or take an exam during the time they are supposed to be at work. It is equally important to be aware of any scheduling changes throughout the semester. For example, is the Tuesday before Thanksgiving a Thursday schedule? Is the Monday after Martin Luther King, Jr. day a Monday schedule? There may be holidays when classes aren't held but the library is open. It is much easier for you to communicate to students that work schedules will mirror the daily schedule of classes than it is for you to deal with students who have legitimately "forgotten" what day of the week it is. It is also much more fair and easier for students if you adopt this practice.

> Know the schedule of semester holidays and breaks of the schools your students attend so that you can adjust the work schedule accordingly.

CONCLUSION

Investing time in preparing a vacancy toolkit can have huge payoffs in the reduction of time it takes to hire students, particularly during busy times of the semester. While your toolkit may need minor revisions every year, it is a small amount of work compared with starting the hiring process from scratch each year. By outlining the process, you ultimately reduce the time spent on hiring to the actual hiring efforts of résumé review, interviewing, reference checking, and so on, which are more important details to focus on when improving your student worker program. Keep the process organized and it will run efficiently.

EXERCISES

EXERCISE 3-1: HIRING CHECKLIST

Customize the hiring checklist to meet your hiring needs.

EXERCISE 3-2: JOB DESCRIPTION TEMPLATE

Use the following template to create job descriptions for each unique job held by a student assistant in your department.

Job Title:	
Competencies:	
Tasks (including percentages):	
Special Physical Requirements:	
Wage:	

REFERENCES

Baldwin, David A., Frances C. Wilkinson, and Daniel C. Barkley. *Effective Management of Student Employment: Organizing for Student Employment in Academic Libraries*. Englewood, CO: Libraries Unlimited, 2000.

Gieseke, Joan. "Performance Appraisal." In *Practical Help for New Supervisors*. Edited by Joan Giesecke. Chicago: American Library Association. 1992.

Slagell, Jeff, and Jeanne Langendorfer. "Don't Tread on Me: The Art of Supervising Student Assistants." *The Serials Librarian* 44 (2003): 279–284.

Stueart, Robert D., and Barbara B. Moran. *Library and Information Center Management*, 5th edition. Englewood, CO: Libraries Unlimited, 1998.

4 RECRUITING AND RESPONDING TO CANDIDATES

MAXIMIZING THE CANDIDATE POOL

Having a job vacancy does not guarantee that you will receive an applicant who meets your needs. Execute an all-out recruiting effort to maximize the chances that you will receive qualified applicants. Recruiting includes advertising your job vacancy and managing the responses to your advertising efforts. Advertising should be attractive and jargon free and clearly state why someone would want the job. Whether you receive too many or too few applicants, knowing how to manage the application process will ensure you make the best possible hires.

ATTRACT ALL POSSIBLE APPLICANTS

Once your new job has been approved, funding has been secured, and you have a strong job description, the next step is to ensure that enough qualified people apply for the job. Having a large applicant pool increases the likelihood of interviewing some terrific candidates, and raising the quality of applicants increases your ability to hire someone well suited and well qualified for the job. The best way to increase the number of applicants you receive is to make the job eye-catching and attractive to potential applicants. Your job ad should present the job in the best possible light yet be honest about the tasks involved. It should make the job sound irresistible to the types of people you want to apply. The primary rule in writing a job ad is to know your audience. Are you trying to attract graduate students? Undergraduates? English majors? Future engineers? Someone who has great public service potential? Your job ad may vary depending on whom you are trying to hook.

Regardless of the type of person you wish to attract to the job, one thing is certain: library jargon is an automatic turn-off for potential applicants. After all, student workers are, for the most part, 18 to 22 year olds. When you were that age, how much library experience (even as a user) did you have? Probably not much. Did you know what an OPAC was? How familiar were you with union catalogs or database vendors? Including a line

> **I'm not getting any decent applicants for the vacancies I have.**
>
> Take a look at your job ad. Remove any jargon that might be turning off potential applicants and make sure it sounds appealing to college students.

61

like "student needed to search the RLG union catalog" or "affix call number labels, printed out using the Dynix system," can be detrimental to your search for the perfect person. However, simply "translating" these phrases into understandable English is an easy first step toward increasing and improving your applicant pool.

Your job ad serves one function: to get people to apply for the job. It is not a detailed job description or a training document. Many supervisors make the mistake of providing way too much information in the job ad. Keep your descriptions simple enough for your prospective applicants to identify with the job, and catchy enough to make them interesting.

Managers' Roundtable Discussion

Question: How do you ensure that you have enough applicants for your vacancies?

Scott: By using the campus employment office and word of mouth, I've always been able to have enough applicants.

Werner: In my current position, I make sure to advertise positions as widely as possible. I post positions on several Listservs, as well as send them to other institutions or programs where I believe potential candidates might be.

Bonnie: By asking faculty, staff, and current students for recommendations, we have always had enough applicants.

Conni: I worried about having enough applicants at first, but the worry didn't last long at all: We always had more applicants than I could begin to interview. Another thing that helps is to ask your current student assistants for referrals.

Michael: Since our hiring process is centralized by the administrative office, I work closely with them to make our departmental needs known. By being familiar with the flow of the semester financial aid notification schedules and class scheduling, I can be sure to communicate with the administrative office when they are receiving the most applicants. I need to hire many students across several departments, so I have learned to be in the right place at the right time with the department that does our hiring.

Gary: We advertise on our Web site, through the student employment office, and ask present employees to tell their friends to come in to fill out a job application.

Nick: Normally, having enough applicants isn't a problem. The library provides a good student worker wage (over $US12.00/hour), so we often have many applicants.

Scott Hanscom, Johns Hopkins University
Werner Haun, Library of Congress
Bonnie Hines, Louisiana State University of Alexandria
Conni Kitten, Texas Tech University Libraries

Michael Miller, Queens College—City University of New York
Gary Ploski, Sarah Lawrence College
Nick Rizzo, University of British Columbia

MAKING ADVERTISING IRRESISTIBLE

You want to make your job eye-catching and really meaningful to the type of person you are trying to recruit. Be careful to avoid shop talk and be certain to use active language. The three keys to a successful ad are knowing your audience, advertising the benefits the job has to offer, and describing the job in a way that potential applicants know the kind of work experience they will gain. Introduce the descriptive elements in the job ad with phrases like, "We will train you to . . ." or "This job is ideal for someone who . . ." to be sure you don't scare off any great potential applicants who feel inadequate for not knowing how to perform specialized library tasks.

PLAY TO YOUR AUDIENCE

Know your audience, and choose language that is appropriate to that audience. Don't launch into a detailed description of the tasks the person you hire will perform or use any library jargon at all. Students will not know what you are talking about, feel inadequate, or otherwise uncomfortable, and that puts you in danger of losing them as potential applicants. After all, no one needs to have heard of OCLC to learn how to do some basic database searching.

Furthermore, an understanding of generational differences can be very helpful toward recruiting the type of student workers you need in your

> Make the job advertisement eye-catching.

Tired Old Language	Exciting, Active, Eye-catching Language
Check in/check out books	Assist patrons at a busy public service desk
Search OCLC, RLIN, and Docline	We will train you to search library databases
Shelve books	Maintain order of library collection
Stock guides	Ensure library patrons have adequate resources
Follow current music cataloging standards (AACR2, MARC, NAF, LCSH, etc.)	In adherence with national standards, write descriptions of recorded materials

Figure 4-1. Writing an Eye-Catching Job Ad

workplace. Traditionally aged college students today, the Millennial Generation, are interested in serving their communities. Describing the "Campus Service" aspects of a library job vacancy may increase your applicant pool (DeBard, 2004: 36). Similarly, knowing that Millennials see work as a learning opportunity, feel comfortable working in teams, desire structure, and like being friends with coworkers can also provide angles for your job ad or suggest aspects to highlight (Legault, 2003: 24).

EMPHASIZE THE BENEFITS/ADVANTAGES

Obviously, you are not offering standard fringe benefits like health insurance or a retirement plan to your student assistants. But, even without knowing it, you are offering advantages to your student workers beyond the hourly wage you pay. To determine what the benefits are, ask your current student workers what they like about working in the department. One common benefit expressed is that working in the library has helped them to understand how to be a more effective library user, and therefore, a more successful student. Your own current student workers may reveal other things they have found to be beneficial about working in your area (aside from the paycheck!). It can be really effective to include this information in your job ads. Working in the library may offer other benefits such as a flexible work schedule, convenient on-campus location, enhanced library privileges, preferential parking, or a guaranteed summer job. For example, the library at Middlesex Community College in Massachusetts offers vouchers, which may be used to cover the cost of tuition and fees, in exchange for work at the college library. Be sure to put anything in the job ad that might make it more attractive to potential student workers.

LINK EXPERIENCE WITH CAREER GOALS

Students want jobs that will provide them with experience that will help them in their intended career field. The more universal (i.e., not library specific) you make the job advertisement sound, the better your chances are of attracting someone who is interested in acquiring that type of experience. Highlight the aspects of the job that are applicable to other positions. For example, highlighting the customer service aspects of a circulation position or the financial record-keeping aspects of an acquisitions job could help you to attract people interested in using these skills in their careers. After all, there is a great amount of competition for the good applicants, both on and off campus. How can you make your job seem more attractive than working at the Gap or waiting tables? Keep in mind that your primary goal is to get a large response to your ad so you can pick the best possible workers. Make your job ad sound irresistible to your audience. You may want to road-test it with current student workers at the library, by

Lackluster job ad:	Transformed into:
Student wanted with ability to do detailed work in following established procedures, ability to work independently, use good judgment in pursuing search strategies in problem solving, ability to communicate effectively and work in a team environment. Job Responsibilities include: preparation of materials in all formats and numerous languages for processing, verification of receipt of orders, process vendor returns, input data into integrated library system Endeavor Voyager, bibliographic searching in various online databases, some clerical functions as assigned.	The Gunner Library Acquisitions Department, responsible for purchasing 200,000 books, CDs, and music scores annually for the Gunner library, is seeking a student to assist us (part-time, flexible daytime hours). We will train you to assist with all aspects of the materials ordering, receiving, and payment processes. This is an ideal job for a business student who wishes to gain work experience with purchasing and financial record keeping.
Lackluster job ad:	Transformed into:
Student with bachelor's degree in music, or degree in progress with experience performing in a variety of musical ensembles and a familiarity with a variety of types of music (classical, popular, avant-garde) wanted to catalog music CDs by replacing and editing records found in online bibliographic databases (RLIN, OCLC, GEAC Advance), following current music cataloging standards (AACR2, MARC, NAF, LCSH, etc.), familiarity with several Western languages preferred.	Music student with performance experience wanted for part-time work in the Barcroft Library Cataloging Department. If you are familiar with a variety of musical styles (everything from classical to avant-garde) we will train you to search a variety of online tools to copy and add records for music recordings to our own library database. Students who have studied or speak one or more foreign language are particularly encouraged to apply.

Figure 4-2. Job Ad Transformed

asking them to read over the draft of the job ad, and asking them how you can make it more appealing to potential applicants.

TIMING THE ADVERTISING

Obviously, the time to advertise your job is when you need someone, or preferably, just before the need arises. However, keep in mind that students, particularly those entering your college or university for the first time, are likely to have a level of excitement about the beginning of the academic year a month or two before it actually starts. If you know for certain that you have some student positions to fill for the beginning of the school year, it's a good idea to post your jobs three to six weeks before the semester begins. While many students will not yet know their class schedule or may otherwise not be ready to commit to the job, some will be, and

> If the hiring process is controlled by someone else, make sure that person or department clearly understands your staffing needs.

those can be hired and possibly trained prior to the beginning-of-semester rush. Hiring and training one or two students prior to the first week of school can be immensely helpful because they will not only be up and running by the first day of school, but they may also be able to assist you with training other new hires.

Talk to your institution's financial aid office and learn when financial aid awards go out. Students are in a job-seeking frame of mind when they receive their financial aid award letters, which detail the amount of federal work study funds that has been allotted to them, so it is in your best interest to make sure your job ad is available at that time. If your job ad is handy to them (either posted on your university's web site or included with the letter) at the time they receive their work study notification, it gives you an advantage over managers who do not have jobs posted at this crucial time.

There is a common misunderstanding that students are only interested in securing employment at the beginning of the school year. While the students who seek jobs mid-semester may be less likely to have a federal work study award, keep in mind that some students, even those with work study awards, wish to get used to their workload and classes before they begin to look for a part-time job. Additionally, students' financial situations can fluctuate through the year. Whenever you determine you need a student worker, don't assume that no one will be interested in the job you need to fill because of the time of year. Human Resources professionals have seen that students inquire about jobs on a weekly (if not daily) basis in some colleges and universities. When you need someone, post a clear, interesting job ad and someone will apply.

Depending on the size of your institution, your library may have its own Human Resources department, which takes responsibility for advertising student positions at the library. If this is the case at your institution, it's the place to start when you need to hire someone. At some institutions, departmental supervisors do not have control over the hiring process, and at the beginning of the school year, a crop of student workers simply shows up at the department's doorstep. If this is the case where you work, you may not be immediately able to make your own hiring decisions. Identify which department (central Human Resources, Financial Aid, etc.) does make hiring decisions and work with them to be sure that you get the candidates you need. Even though you may not have immediate control over your hires, it is your responsibility to communicate to the people doing the hiring exactly what you need. For example, if you need people who have the tolerance for stress required for working at a busy public service desk, see if the hiring department will ask specific questions that gauge a candidate's tolerance for stress. If you are looking for someone who has tremendous attention to detail, talk to the hiring department to stress the importance of them screening applicants for this trait. Not being able to make your own hiring decisions is, admittedly, a frustrating situation. Anyone can complain about it, but a smart manager will be sure their hiring needs are understood by the people making the hiring decisions. It is important to get the people who do the hiring to understand your need. Inviting them to your department to see what it is you do can help them better understand the types of students you want to hire.

Figure 4-3. Gain More Control over the Hiring Process

RESPONDING TO JOB ADVERTISEMENT RESULTS

Once you've posted your job advertisements, one of three things will happen:

1. You will receive the perfect amount of responses, which would be the exact number as the vacancies you have, and each and every one would be perfectly qualified for the job for which you are hiring

2. You will receive far too few responses, and not enough will be from applicants that are qualified for the job for which you are hiring.

3. You will be inundated with responses to the point that it is overwhelming to even contemplate reviewing them to find suitable candidates.

While it would be great if you received résumés from three perfect candidates for the three job openings that you have, it's probably not a realistic prediction of what will happen. It is far more likely you'll receive either too few or too many applications.

INCREASING APPLICANT POOLS EXPONENTIALLY

If you do not receive enough (or any) applicants for the job you need to fill, take another look at your job as advertised. How attractive is it? Did you sneak some jargon in? Is your pay scale comparable to other jobs on campus? Your job ad may need revision to bring in the response you want.

Another way to find qualified candidates is by referrals. Don't forget to ask the students who work in your department if they know of anyone looking for a job. Good student workers are not likely to recommend someone unless they feel that the person would be a good worker. Talk to your colleagues, as they may have good student workers who can recommend people they know, or perhaps your colleagues have excellent student workers whose schedules they can no longer accommodate.

If you still can't find qualified candidates, it's time to get creative. Does your campus have a job fair? Some managers have had good luck posting their job ads as flyers within the library or around campus. One department at a large public university, frustrated by the channels available to them to find qualified candidates, set up an informational table outside of a campus dining commons and found several attractive candidates. Brainstorm ways to recruit candidates. It may also be helpful to talk to colleagues about how they handled underwhelming responses, and use some of the suggestions they offer.

Ted Lawton, the former stacks supervisor at New York University's Bobst Library, was faced with the problem of too few applicants back in the middle 1980s. He could not get enough NYU students to apply for jobs reshelving books in the stacks, and those that he was able to hire he could not retain. Ted suspects that the general prosperity that the country was enjoying at that time meant that most NYU students were able to afford attending college without work being a financial necessity. Whatever the cause, he was faced with a problem. During that time, the stacks department was responsible for shelving 800,000 volumes annually. The stacks department simply was not able to get the books back on the shelves in a timely way because they never had enough people on staff. The library experimented with hiring temporary workers and with hiring people in special job re-entry programs, experiments that Ted describes as disastrous. Ted's solution was to hire local high school students as stacks assistants. This idea was met with much skepticism among library management, who questioned the abilities and work ethics of such a young staff. Growing up himself in an urban setting, Ted understood that a strong desire for a job could serve as an effective motivator. While the Bobst Stacks Department now employs a mix of NYU students and high school students, the high school students, who receive course credit in addition to minimum wage, remain an integral part of the team. Ted, who has since been promoted to stacks manager, admits that high-school-age workers do require more supervision, and that is perhaps the biggest challenge of the program. However, the program continues to meet the library's needs.

HANDLING OVERWHELMING RESPONSE GRACEFULLY

Believe it or not, it is also possible to receive too many responses to a job ad. How many is too many? That all depends on the person reviewing the applications, but too many is the number that stresses you out and makes you not want to begin reviewing applications because you can't imagine getting through them all. One way to manage the number of responses you receive is to include detailed instructions on how to apply for the job in the job ad. Including a sentence like, "please e-mail your resume plus the names and contact information for three references," can be a highly useful tool. First of all, it will ensure that you have the information you need to make an informed decision on whom you wish to interview. Secondly, if you are looking for someone who can follow directions well (and you should be), including such directions will help to weed out unqualified applicants. It is like administering a test: if you ask applicants to include certain information in their application package, and they fail to do so, that

---

Help—I have 150 applicants in my inbox. What do I do?

Automatically weed out the ones who didn't submit that application the way you asked. If you wanted them to send their class schedule, and three references, e-mail from anyone who didn't can be automatically deleted.

Method	Advantages	Disadvantages
Submit in person	You can check out the applicant with minimal time investment. You can put a face with a name.	If you receive several applicants, this can get time-consuming. Applicants may stop by at inopportune times, times when you are not available, etc. You may get lots of people stopping by even after you fill the vacancy.
Phone first	Allows for pre-interview screening. Can remind applicants to provide references and other information you may need.	You may find yourself answering the same question over and over again. People may not reach you and you may have lots of phone calls to return. If you receive several applicants, this can get time-consuming. You may get lots of people stopping by even after you fill the vacancy.
E-mail	You can be very specific in your job ad, and use that as a means to reduce the number of unqualified applicants. You can easily manage the "rejections" after you fill the job.	You may feel obligated to respond to all e-mails.

Figure 4-4. Application Methods

automatically disqualifies them for the job. After all, if someone can't follow simple instructions, do you really want them working in your department? By including such a requirement in the job ad, you are giving yourself license to discard any applications you receive that do not include all of the information you ask for. Supervisors who have followed this advice have been able to reduce an applicant pool of over 75 students to a manageable group of 25 qualified applicants who can follow directions.

Be clear in your job ad how you want people to apply for the job. Do you want them to submit their application in person? Do you want them to e-mail a resume? Do you want them to phone for a brief telephone screening before you look through their application? Every manager is going to have a preferred method. All methods have advantages and disadvantages, but e-mail is the most efficient use of time.

Keep in mind that you are also not under any obligation to read every application you receive, or speak to every student who drops by to ask about the job. Your goal is to hire qualified applicants who are likely to do well in the position. If you can do that by only reading the first ten résumés you receive, there is no reason to continue to review applicants.

> Use the application instructions as a mini-quiz on attention to detail—ask applicants to submit the application in a certain way. Those that disregard your instructions may not be students you wish to hire.

After all, hiring student workers may be a big part of your job and your top priority at the start of the school year, but it is probably not your only responsibility.

CONCLUSION

The way you advertise can make or break your recruitment efforts. The job ad is your opportunity to sell the job to potential applicants, so make it sound irresistible, by choosing the language carefully, highlighting the benefits of the job, and underscoring the job's learning opportunities. If you receive too many applicants, give yourself permission to review only those you need to. If you receive too few applicants, rework your job ad, or get creative. Remember that creating an effective student assistant program is a building process. "As you build your program your reputation as a great place to work will become known, making it easier to hire in the future" (Slagell and Langendorfer, 2003: 280).

EXERCISES

EXERCISE 4-1: REWRITING THE JOB ADVERTISEMENT

Grab a copy of the job ad and rewrite it. If you don't have one, start from scratch with your list of job competencies and tasks, and make your job ad irresistible.

EXERCISE 4-2: INCREASE CONTROL OVER THE HIRING PROCESS

Write up a description of the qualities a student worker needs to have in order to be successful at each job in your area. Share this information with any external department that is involved in your hiring process.

REFERENCES

DeBard, Michael. "Millennials Coming to College." *New Directions for Student Services* 106 (Summer 2004): 33–45.

Legault, Marie. "Caution: Mixed Generations at Work." *Canadian HR Reporter* 16, 21 (December 1, 2003): 23–24.

Slagell, Jeff, and Jeanne Langendorfer. "Don't Tread on Me: The Art of Supervising Student Assistants." *The Serials Librarian* 44 (2003): 279–284.

Wilson, Christine, and John Folz. "Managing Multiple Generations at Work." *Feed and Grain* 44 (August /September 2005): 54–60.

5 INTERVIEWING AND SELECTING CANDIDATES

WHY CONDUCT A FORMAL INTERVIEW?

I don't have time to interview all of the qualified candidates—can't I skip this step?

No. It's really important to interview the most *qualified candidates*. You don't have to interview every qualified candidate. Each interview can take as little as 20 minutes, which is a worthwhile investment of your time. If you legitimately don't have 20 minutes for each of 4–10 interviews, delegate the interviewing to someone else.

Hiring decisions are some of the most important you will make as a manager, so make them with the best information possible. Engaging in a formal interview process for any vacancy, including student positions, ensures that you will have the information you need to make an informed choice about whom you hire. The formal interview process involves conducting competency-based interviews (also known as behavior-based interviews) of qualified applicants, utilizing objective screening methods and checking references for each of the top applicants. Keeping the process formal impresses upon student applicants the importance of the commitment they are making.

GUIDELINES FOR CONSTRUCTING INTERVIEW QUERIES

The student employment planning described thus far leads up to the interview stage of the hiring process. By the time you are ready to conduct interviews, you will have completed job and workflow audits, identified job competencies, received approval for the new job(s), and obtained funding necessary to support any new positions. Ensuring that the interview process concludes with the hire of individuals who will be successful in the positions is only possible with a well-planned interview. Before the interview, identify what the goal of the interview is. Are you attempting to narrow the applicant pool? Do you wish to find someone with superior customer service skills (thinking other skills can be taught)? Are you interested in finding a candidate with high skills in three distinct areas? (Rimmer, 1992: 6) Having a clearly articulated goal for interviewing will help you to achieve what you set out to do.

> Understand that a formal interview helps the student to understand the commitment he or she is making and helps to raise the bar on performance expectations.

Are you the most appropriate person to interview potential candidates? The person who will be directly supervising the new hire should do the bulk of the interviewing, so if you are not that person, work with that person to be sure they run the interview appropriately. The interviewer should not waste valuable interview time asking questions that are covered in the applicants résumé or cover letter, or to which you already know the answer (Rimmer, 1992: 6). Plan for the following facets of the interview:

1. Question the candidate thoroughly
2. Question the candidate professionally
3. Question the candidate fairly
4. Question the candidate legally
5. Question the candidate comfortably and thoughtfully

QUESTION THOROUGHLY

While it is not necessary to review all of the work you have done thus far when preparing for interviews, it is essential to review the job competencies, and derive interview questions from them. Remember that past behavior is a good predictor of job performance. So, asking, "Tell me about a situation that was particularly challenging for you" will lead to better information about the candidate than asking, "What challenges you?" Asking behavior-based questions also keeps the process objective.

Job competencies should lead directly into interview questions. The easy formula for writing job interview questions is simply to look at the list of competencies, and add the phrase "tell me about a time when you . . ." to the front of each competency. That way, you'll be asking questions that address past experiences, actions, and accomplishments. Ask for examples of how the candidate behaved in key situations on the job. By asking for

Essential Job Competency:	Interview Question:
Teamwork	"Describe an experience working in a group toward a common goal."
Customer focused	"Please give me an example of when you exceeded someone's expectations."
Attention to detail	"Tell me about something you have done where you had to pay really close attention to get it right."

Figure 5-1. Job Competencies and Related Interview Questions

specific examples, you are ensuring that you are making a good hire, and protecting yourself from hiring someone who simply "interviews well."

When interviewing students, it is entirely possible that they have not had jobs before. If they can't provide you with an example of how they have dealt with a difficult customer, try to broaden the scope of the question. If they have never dealt with a difficult customer, perhaps they have had a misunderstanding with a teacher. If they have never had a job that required attention to detail, perhaps one of their classes did. If they have never "worked" as part of a team, perhaps they have experienced playing a team sport or being involved in a club. If their limited experience stops them from proving a specific example, ask them for a hypothetical answer. Probe their answers with follow-up questions such as:

> Write effective interview questions by placing the phrase "Tell me about a time when you . . ." in front of each essential skill of the job. For example, "Tell me about a time when you had to pay close attention to detail," or, "Tell me about a time when you worked as part of a team or group."

"How did you first get involved with X?"

"What happened next?"

"Could you elaborate on that?"

"What did you learn from that?"

"What did you actually do?"

"What did you actually say?"

"How did it turn out? What was the result?"

Listen to the answers for the thought or motivation behind the action, as that can tell you a good deal about who the candidate is and the quality of work you can expect from him or her. If the candidate does not answer the question adequately, or does not answer the question asked, try re-phrasing the question (Rimmer, 1992: 10; Kalinsky and Plummer, 2000).

What interests you about working here?

Describe your experience with libraries.

Tell me about a time when you had to keep calm under pressure.

Tell me about a time when you had to pay close attention to detail?

Why did you choose your particular major?

What would be your ideal first job when you graduate?

Describe your work at your last job?

What did you like best about your job at _____?

What did you like least about your job at _____?

What is your idea of challenging work?

How would you react if assigned a task you really didn't like?

Where do you see yourself in 10 years?

Figure 5-2. Sample Interview Questions

I always feel so awkward when interviewing candidates that I'm sure the candidate picks up on it. How can I stop this from happening?

Ask a trusted colleague, or even one of you current student assistants, to engage in a role-play of an interview. Practice can really help to improve your interview skills.

Other staff, the new student hire's prospective coworkers, may be involved if that sort of involvement is the culture in your organization. Involving staff is a good idea if they will work particularly closely with a small number of students, or if staff have been concerned about the process. In some workplaces, it may not be possible to involve all, or even some staff in the process. When hiring large numbers of students, it may not be practical. Certainly, if staff are involved in the interview process, the most efficient way to do this is for a group of staff to meet each student applicant, rather than the interviewee meeting each staffer individually. Involving staff can be a good way to get their buy-in for hiring a student.

QUESTION PROFESSIONALLY

Conducting an actual, sit-down job interview helps potential student workers understand the commitment they are making. It helps them to understand that you are talking about a real job for which they must meet certain expectations if they wish to receive the privilege of a paycheck. Andy Spackman, circulation manager at Brigham Young University, agrees. "We hire clerks through the university's hiring system. But our Team Leader and backroom students are always hired in-house. Nevertheless, we still follow a formal hiring procedure for those positions, posting job openings, taking applications, and interviewing candidates. This encourages the students to take the process seriously when they apply for promotion." Even internal candidates should be put through an interview process. That way,

The best predictor of future performance is past performance. Competency-based interviewing is a strategy that allows employers to learn about the past performance of potential employees to gauge how that past performance fits the skills necessary to be successful at the given job. Competency-based interviewing helps the interviewer to focus on how the potential employee has learned from experiences, rather than focus on the nuts and bolts of education and experience—which have already been clearly defined in the applicant's résumé. By asking the interviewee about actual experiences he or she has had, or choices he or she has made, the interviewer gets a much better feel for who the interviewee actually is, and what he or she can bring to the position. Rather than giving the candidate an opportunity to provide rote answers to overused interview questions like, "Describe your strengths and weaknesses," competency-based interviewing gives the candidate an opportunity to provide thoughtful answers based on his or her actual experience.

Figure 5-3. Competency-Based Interviewing

you'll have notes from interviews to back up your decision, which is particularly important if some candidates are internal and others are not. Plus, it endorses the formality of the process and emphasizes the importance of the job commitment for all candidates regardless of how well they know you or the institution.

QUESTION FAIRLY

Make sure you make a list of appropriate, non-leading competency-based interview questions in advance, as well as a basic outline of what you want to be sure you say during the interview. Review each candidate's résumé prior to the meeting, so you can follow up on any information on the résumé that is unclear to you. Print several copies of your outline (one for each interview you will conduct), including questions, leaving room to make notes on the outline itself, so that you have a script to follow and a place to take notes during each interview. Because you may interview several students, it is important to take brief, factual notes during the interview so that you can remember which students are the best candidates. Don't worry about writing down everything the candidate says (this can be really distracting for the applicant) but write down just enough to help you to recall the candidate's responses. Reserve your judgments until you have met with all candidates, and certainly don't write any judgments on your interview notes to protect you and your organization from any legal liability. All interviewees should be asked the same questions to be sure that all are being reviewed on the same criteria. This will help you to make an informed choice, and will also be fair to the student applicants.

QUESTION LEGALLY

Keep your employment inquiries legal. Personal information should never be discussed during an interview, even if the applicant is the person who brings up the topic, or if the topic is related to the job somehow. For instance, avoid questions regarding religion or days of religious observance. Instead, state to all applicants the days, hours, and shifts available, or ask all applicants to provide you with the hours they would be available to work, and don't go into the reasons why or why not regarding other times. Don't ask applicants if they have any physical disabilities or about their health; instead, share the job description with all applicants and ask if they can perform the essential functions. Never discuss race, national origin, religious affiliation or beliefs, sexual orientation, family responsibilities, disabilities, or criminal history. If an applicant brings up illegal information, simply say, "That information is not relevant. Let's focus a bit more on your work experience" (Kalinsky and Plummer, 2000).

> A candidate I interviewed started talking about her religious affiliations. I know that this topic isn't legal in an interview, but I didn't know how to make her stop talking about it!
>
> Simply say, "That information isn't relevant to the interview. Let's focus on your work experience." Then, immediately follow up that statement with a competency-based interview question.

Do	Don't
Ask competency-based questions.	Harshly judge the candidate or fail to recognize that each individual has stylistic differences.
Get back to competency-based questions if a candidate volunteers illegal information by saying something like, "That's not really relevant. Let's focus on your work experience and how it relates to this job."	Ask questions of a personal nature (about race, physical disability, religious beliefs or observances, age, sexual orientation, marital status, children, national origin, etc.).
Show respect for the candidate and try to put him or her at ease.	Try to "stick it to them" or intentionally make things tricky or difficult.
Turn off your office phone, cell phone, and conduct the interview in a room behind closed doors and free of interruption.	Get distracted by interruptions, other work, or even evaluative thoughts about the candidate.
Allow the candidate to talk.	Answer your own questions, interrupt, or monopolize the interview.

Figure 5-4. Interview Dos and Don'ts

Managers' Roundtable Discussion

Question: What are some red flags you've seen during interviews and/or reference checks?

Scott: During the interview I look for punctuality, attentiveness, and what kinds of questions they ask. If I decide to check a reference, and it isn't extremely positive, I take it as a red flag.

Werner: Lack of attentiveness during the interview is the biggest red flag I have experienced with students. In conducting reference checks, we use a standard list of questions that, among other issues, address an applicant's attendance and dependability. If problems arise or are found in either of these areas I hesitate in hiring them.

Bonnie: Because all of our students are recommended by faculty, staff, or current students, we don't conduct reference checks. But, during interviews, I have seen some red flags, like poor eye contact, careless personal hygiene, bringing a third party to the interview or other bizarre behavior (one applicant walked around my desk and opened a file drawer during an interview).

Conni: A red flag during an interview might be a complacent attitude. Also, if the person doesn't seem to be customer-service-oriented, energetic, or work-oriented, those would be red flags. A big red flag during a reference check is that the person you're talking to is neutral and will only tell you that the potential employee worked there during a certain time.

Michael: After the students have been vetted by the administrative office, the area supervisors and I get a chance to speak with and start training them. I find that inexact or unspecific responses to questions are usually indicators of who we will not be able to rely upon as time goes by.

Gary: One red flag I have encountered during an interview is a candidate's inability to listen to/hear a question I ask. Instead of reacting to a question I ask a student responds to another thought they have about the position. I'm also wary of someone who does not maintain clean personal hygiene.

(Cont'd.)

Managers' Roundtable Discussion *(Continued)*

Nick: The biggest red flags during an interview is answering questions with "I think I can do that . . ." rather than "I can do that." Through past experience, I've found that students who are hesitant in their replies often end up being unable to follow through on their promises/commitments (e.g., I've had students who hesitantly say that they will commit to working the entire academic year, but then end up quitting halfway through). During reference checks, I listen to what the reference doesn't say. Any hesitation is a real red flag.

Question: Do you ever use objective screening methods, like quizzes or work simulations, in your selection process?

Scott: No.

Werner: When I was being interviewed for my first student assistant position, I was given a manual dexterity test to determine if I had the necessary hand skills to perform conservation work. If you have a choice of students, testing might be a good method to use to help in the selection process.

Bonnie: We have not used this approach.

Conni: No, but what a good idea!

Michael: We use Library of Congress call number testing as part of the training process, but not the screening process.

Gary: We do not use quizzes at present, but this is something I intend to develop.

Nick: Yes, I use call number tests for applicants with previous library experience, and I use a short accuracy test for all applicants.

Scott Hanscom, Johns Hopkins University	Michael Miller, Queens College—City University
Werner Haun, Library of Congress	of New York
Bonnie Hines, Louisiana State University of Alexandria	Gary Ploski, Sarah Lawrence College
Conni Kitten, Texas Tech University Libraries	Nick Rizzo, University of British Columbia

QUESTION COMFORTABLY AND THOUGHTFULLY

At the beginning of the interview, start out with some small talk on topics like the weather or if they had any trouble finding your office or when they moved into their dormitory or what classes they are taking. This can help the candidate to relax and feel more at ease. Introduce yourself at the beginning of the interview, and explain a little bit about how the interview will be conducted. For example, say something like, "The interview will take about 20 minutes, I'll ask you some questions about your job experiences and then I'll give you a chance to ask questions about the job." While you are ultimately interested in finding out about the applicant, you also want to spend a little bit of effort selling the job and workplace, so certainly be kind and courteous to the applicant and tell them the benefits of working in the library. After all, if the applicant is excellent, you want to make sure that the interview has been a positive experience for him or her or he or she will not want to accept the job. Try to put the applicant at ease so he or she can be relaxed enough to provide you with thoughtful, honest answers. Understand that interviewing is a two-way process. While the candidate should do most of the talking the interview also serves as a forum for you to continue to sell the job to the potential candidate as well as a time for the candidate to get his or her questions about the job answered (Rimmer, 1992: 5).

As you conclude the interview, be sure to give the candidate an opportunity to ask questions. Provide the applicant with your contact information should he or she think of questions over the next few days. Explain the next steps in the decision-making process and thank the applicant for coming in to meet with you. Tours and extensive introductions are not necessary at this point. Remember, this is the interview, a time to decide if you want to hire the student, not an orientation session.

Immediately after the interview, read over your notes and flesh out anything that needs more detail. Once you have conducted all of the planned interviews, collected reference checks, and administered any quizzes or other screening methods, you can compare the full package for each applicant and make your hiring decisions.

> Ask competency-based questions first, before describing the job in detail. If you begin the interview by discussing the specifics of the job you risk hiring someone who simply interviews well.

SCREENING OBJECTIVELY

Many human resources experts believe that most hiring decisions are based on inefficient hiring methods, including an overemphasized reliance on the training or experience a candidate has received in previous jobs or through formal education. Focusing on these points places too little attention on a candidate's actual skills and potential for success on the job (Zeller, 2005: 42). Instead, experts advocate assessing candidates based on objective methods, such as work samples (simulations of workplace activities), structured interviews (in which all candidates are asked the same questions), intelligence tests, or personality tests (Lin and Kleiner, 2004: 112; Patterson, 2000: 79; Zeller, 2005: 47). While the latter two suggestions are most likely neither feasible nor appropriate in a student assistant program, quizzes or exercises administered as part of the selection process can be helpful, *objective* ways to gain more information about the candidates' abilities. Asking shelving applicants to put a few books in call number order (after giving them a basic overview of the classification system) or giving them a list of words to alphabetize can help you to determine their aptitude for that type of work. A colleague of mine had great success devising a PowerPoint exercise simulating work at the library entrance. Students staffing the entrance had to be familiar with a large variety of ID cards which made the job stressful in its repetition and boredom.

Using this PowerPoint, he was able to hire only those students who had both the highest tolerance for repetition and the best attention to detail. If a student worker's job involves using foreign language skills, it would be appropriate to give the applicants a short translation or transliteration quiz. If a job requires strong attention to detail, administering a quiz with detailed directions or multiple steps may be helpful in identifying the best qualified applicants.

In an article addressed to managers in government organizations, Shawn Zeller draws on research published in leading psychology journals when he presents objective screening methods as a much greater predictor of future success than factors such as training, years of job experience, or grade point average (Zeller, 2005: 42). In fact, the work sample test has a 29 percent correlation to job success, as compared with grade point average, which has a 4 percent correlation to job success. While testing should never be the only criteria used in hiring decisions, it can be a very effective way to weed out unsuitable candidates or determine for which projects or tasks a new hire is best suited (Patterson, 2000: 78).

CHECKING REFERENCES

Always check references before you hire. It is absolutely essential to get outside verification on any individual you plan to hire. Obtain the names of three people who can serve as references from each applicant. Some supervisors prefer to check references prior to conducting interviews, because it saves both your time and the time of the applicant. Other supervisors wait until they have a short list of applicants before they check references. When you check references is really up to you, but don't skip this important step.

CHOOSE YOUR REFERENCE QUESTIONS CAREFULLY

When checking references, ask the reference questions about his or her relationship to the applicant and how long he or she has known the applicant, as well as questions about the applicant's job performance and reliability. Figure 5-5 provides an outline and worksheet for checking references. References are an essential part of the hiring decision. They can help to corroborate your own judgments of the candidate, and can be a valuable sounding board for you to investigate any issues or questions on which you would like an additional opinion. Some organizations, however, have strict regulations about providing references, and individuals contacted may not be able to provide detailed references. I am not a lawyer, but my understanding from lawyers is that organizations are afraid of lawsuits on two

Name of Candidate_____ Date_____

Position Applied For_____

Reference_____ Phone_____

1. How do you know the applicant?

2. How long have you known the applicant?

3. Could you please comment on his or her punctuality.

4. Could you please comment on his or her attendance.

5. Could you please comment on the quality of his or her work.

6. Would you hire_____again?

7. Is there anything else I should know?

Figure 5-5. Reference Checking Worksheet

| Always check references before you hire. |

grounds: Defamation of Character and Invasion of Privacy. Defamation of Character occurs when one person makes false statements against another or if the truth is communicated with the intent to do harm to another. Invasion of Privacy occurs when irrelevant personal information is divulged. Because some organizations fear lawsuits on these grounds, they may mandate that references can only verify an individual's dates of employment. That is why it is important to ask applicants to provide a few references, to ensure that at least two will be able to provide you with a detailed reference.

- Reference doesn't call you back
- Candidate supplies an inappropriate person as a reference (e.g., a relative)
- Candidate provides a home number (unless job was domestic in nature or reference has retired)
- Reference simply provides dates of employment
- Something about the individual's tone of voice makes you think he or she is not telling the truth or is hesitant to divulge something
- You have a reservation or feeling that the reference is not being honest or that you are being "scammed"

Figure 5-6. Red Flags during Reference Checks

SELECTING THE BEST PERSON

Once you have reviewed résumés, interviewed candidates, evaluated the results of objective testing, and spoken to references, it is up to you to make the final selections on candidates to whom you extend offers. Be sure not to make hiring decisions based on one tool, but rather weigh all of the information that you have gathered through competency-based interviewing, objective screening tools, and reference checks. Remember what is important to your department and organization. For example, Southwest Airlines "hires for attitude and trains for skill" (Kaye and Jordan-Evans, 2001: 32). Their philosophy is that it is much easier to train someone in the tangible, task-based aspects of a job than to re-train someone's social skills, attitude, or general outlook.

To make a final hiring selection, you simply weigh each candidate's potential for being successful at the job, motivation to perform well, and fit with other members of the department. It may be very tempting to hire a graduate student for their maturity, but graduate students are more difficult to keep challenged and interested than undergraduate students (Slagell and Langendorfer, 2003: 281). How well a candidate's availability matches the hours for which you need coverage is also an important factor in the selection process. Use your judgment. You know the needs of your department and have the expertise to make good decisions.

> **I don't have time to check references—can I skip this step?**
>
> No. Checking references can take as little as 5–10 minutes. It's the best way to know if there will be future problems with an employee. Even if you simply inquire about punctuality and attendance, you may gain information that will help you avoid making the wrong hire.

CONCLUSION

Human resources experts often cite the costs associated with high turnover, which include lost productivity, greater absenteeism, and actual dollar costs associated with filling a vacancy, which, for entry-level staff can approach $7,000 (Zeller, 2005: 42–44). It may be difficult or impossible to assign such a figure to replacing student library staff, but anyone who has ever filled a vacancy knows that it is a time-consuming and labor-intensive process, and it makes sense to hire intelligently. Plan your interviews well. Competency-based interview questions will ensure that interview questions get at the skills you need your new hires to possess. Keep interviews professional, fair, and comfortable, keeping in mind the public relations aspects of the interview. Objective screening methods can be helpful for keeping inquiries legal as well as keeping the interview structured and fair. Reference checks are essential. The whole package of thorough interviewing, objective screening methods, and reference checking will help you to make an informed decision which will lead to the most appropriate students being hired.

EXERCISES

EXERCISE 5-1: INTERVIEW QUESTIONS FOR JOB COMPETENCIES

Write interview questions based on the following identified job competencies:

Competency	Interview Question
Ability to search database(s)	
Experience with bibliographic citations	
Attention to detail	
Ability to provide outstanding customer service, even under pressure	
Tolerance for monotonous tasks	

EXERCISE 5-2: MOCK INTERVIEW

If you are new to interviewing, practice is essential before you begin interviewing for real. Write up your competency-based interview questions and ask a colleague or a current student worker to practice interviewing with you. Ask them for feedback on how you could improve your interview technique.

REFERENCES

Kalinsky, Geri, and Elizabeth Plummer. "Interviewing and Hiring Workshop." Human Resources Division, New York University, 2000. Photocopy.

Kaye, Beverly L., and Sharon Jordan-Evans. "New Hires: Getting the Right Fit." *Credit Union Executive Journal* 41, 2 (March/April 2001): 32–34.

Lin, Yei-Fang, and Brian H. Kleiner. "How to Hire Employees Effectively." *Management Research News* 27, 4/5 (2004): 108–115.

Patterson, Maureen. "Overcoming the Hiring Crunch: Tests Deliver Informed Choices." *Employment Relations Today* 27, 3 (Autumn 2000): 77.

Rimmer, Anne. "Interviewing." In *Practical Help for New Supervisors*. Edited by Joan Giesecke. Chicago: American Library Association, 1992.

Slagell, Jeff, and Jeanne Langendorfer. "Don't Tread on Me: The Art of Supervising Student Assistants." *The Serials Librarian* 44 (2003): 279–284.

Zeller, Shawn. "The Perfect Candidate." *Government Executive* 37, 11 (July 1, 2005): 40–46.

6 TRAINING AND ORIENTING NEW WORKERS

WHY INVEST THE TIME IN TRAINING?

Students will need to be trained to do the job for which they are hired. Training and orientation are the most important investments to make in a student assistant program. Recruiting and selecting appropriate student workers takes time and effort, and to get the most benefit from your efforts, train your new hires thoroughly. To make students feel confident and comfortable in their jobs is one of the most effective ways to improve retention and is accomplished by effective training and orientation. Many aspects of an effective student worker program can be seen as investments; while time-consuming, they have a huge payoff in improving the caliber of students in your employ. Nowhere is this more apparent than with training and orientation, both of which improve the odds for longer retention. If a student worker feels lost on the job—a scenario that is likely without proper training and orientation—he or she isn't likely to continue in the job. If a student isn't properly trained, he or she will make many mistakes and you may not want the student to stick around. Do yourself a favor and do it right the first time.

DEVELOPING STRATEGIES FOR EASY ORIENTATION AND GREAT TRAINING

> Plan a thorough training program for all new hires.

Training consists of communicating to the student worker the steps involved in successfully executing the job, and making sure that the student understands and carries out those steps. Orientation includes providing an overview of the library and an explanation of how the student assistant's tasks fit into the mission of the library and any other information that a student worker needs to be successful and feel comfortable in the job (Halsted and Neely, 1990: 62). Surprisingly, many supervisors do not invest the time necessary to properly train new student hires. A common sentiment

When training a new hire to conduct a job task, provide him or her with the context for why the task is done. For example, when training someone in shelf reading, explain that we commit so much time to shelf reading because users, thinking they are helpful, put the books back on the shelves, and sometimes they put them back in the wrong place. Explaining that a book in the wrong location is as good as lost provides a useful context for staff to understand the importance of what they are doing. Provide a personalized context for even greater understanding—ask the trainee if he or she has ever had the experience of going to the shelf to find a book and seeing the book was missing. Learners respond to a personal context and retain the importance of what they are learning.

Figure 6-1. Importance of Training in Context

among supervisors is that they do not want to "waste their time" training a student who will not have long-term retention. Certainly, training can be an exhausting process for both the student and the manager, especially when done properly. However, a properly trained student assistant is much more likely to achieve job success and a student assistant who feels successful in his or her job is more likely to continue in that job year after year. To minimize the work involved in training, and to ensure the training process is thorough, the following strategies may be helpful:

1. Create a detailed training toolkit
2. Enlist others in training
3. Train actively

EXPLORING THE COMPONENTS OF A TRAINING TOOLKIT

The training toolkit is a packet of documents that you will need to get your newly hired student up to full productivity. Similar to the vacancy toolkit, the purpose of putting the training toolkit together is simply to keep the training and orientation process running smoothly, and to ensure that you do not find yourself reinventing the training process each time you train someone. The training toolkit could be a folder on your computer, filled with electronic documents, or perhaps a paper file including everything you need to make a new hire. The training toolkit could be posted as a Blackboard or WebCT class, so that student workers could access the information as they need it. The format of the training toolkit does not matter. What matters is that the training toolkit exists as one unit, thus eliminating wasted time in collecting all the elements, or worse yet creating those elements when it comes time to train a new hire. The training toolkit is particularly valuable if you are training multiple students at the same time or if training coincides with other busy times in the semester. The training toolkit should consist of a training checklist, an orientation checklist, and all training and orientation materials that each new hire needs.

CREATING A STRUCTURED TRAINING CHECKLIST

While you are training a new student you'll need to verify that a trainee has learned what you are training and the best way to do that is with an informal quiz. One of the most effective tools in training is the training checklist, which you can use to guide your quizzing. A training checklist is a comprehensive document listing all of the workflows a student needs to master during the training period and it includes each and every task a student will need to learn to be successful at the job. Examining the job description can be helpful in determining the elements of the training checklist. To create a training checklist, identify the main job elements from the job description. These elements will become the headings for the training checklist, and represent regular task assignments for the person occupying the position. Then, beneath each heading, write in the steps that someone would need to know to complete each regular task assignment. Figure 6.2 illustrates how to determine the elements of a training checklist from the tasks listed in a job description.

> **It takes forever to train students. What can I do to speed up the process?**
>
> Keep the training as organized as possible. Use a training checklist for each student to remind you what each student still needs to learn. Get help from other people in your unit—even veteran student assistants—and be sure you have good documentation that new hires can read during training. This helps to reinforce policy and procedures and gives you a much needed break.

Task	Competency	%
Charge out material to users in accordance with established **policies and procedures** (includes general checkouts as well as reserve materials, **ILL** materials, **manual** checkouts and **FLA**).	Attention to **detail**, understanding of policy and guidelines, **customer service attitude**, strict adherence **to privacy policy**.	35%
Check in materials.	Attention to **detail**, ability to follow a multi-step process (**check in on system, re-sensitize books, sort materials**), use good judgment when identifying material for **repair**.	35%
Accept fine **payment**, make change, accept payment for ILLs, carrel rental, etc.	Accuracy in handling money, understanding of various payment **types** and procedures thereof, understanding of various categories of service that require payment (e.g., library **memberships, printing cards, copy cards**).	10%

Figure 6-2. The Job Description as a Tool for Devising a Training Checklist

Task	Competency	%
Assist patrons in person and over the **phone**.	Exercise **courtesy** and **judgment** when answering patron queries.	10%
Assist with **room reservations**.	Understand different **policies** that apply to different **categories** of users.	5%
Register **new patron** in accordance with established policies and **procedures**.	Attention to **detail**, typing accuracy, understanding of different **category** of user.	5%

Figure 6-2. The Job Description as a Tool for Devising a Training Checklist (Continued)

If you are new to creating a training checklist, keep in mind that it may take several drafts before you have included all elements of the job. The best way to test the training checklist is to go over it in detail while performing the tasks it is meant to cover. It is also helpful to use it in a mock training exercise with someone who is familiar with the steps involved in each workflow and can provide feedback on the checklist as a training tool. As with the training manual and execution of student training, veteran student assistants can be a valuable resource when compiling and testing the training checklist. You may need to revise and test your training checklist more than once to get it right. Figure 6-3 shows a training checklist for the job described in Figure 6-2.

The training checklist has three basic uses: planning the training, checking efficacy of training, and keeping track of what training still needs to be accomplished. After training on a given job requirement has been executed, use the training checklist to prompt questions of the newly trained individual. For example, several hours or a day after someone has been trained on labeling new acquisitions, sit down with the individual and ask them to explain to you how one labels new acquisitions. Just as in the interviewing stages, asking non-leading questions will ensure you can determine what it is they know and what skill or knowledge gaps may still be present. Repeat this process for each task a student will perform. Sign off on each task when a student has satisfactorily demonstrated that he knows and understands departmental procedures.

DEVELOP A COMPREHENSIVE TRAINING MANUAL

The training manual should include written instructions for everything the employee must do in the course of his or her job. It should also include all details of work expectations as well as orientation information, such as the library's mission statement, dress code, timekeeping regulations, expectations of employment, rest and meal break policies, university closure policy, jury duty, military or other leave policies, grievance policy and any

CIRCULATION SERVICES
LEVEL ONE
CIRCULATION TRAINING CHECKLIST

DATE _____

Trainee _____   Trainer _____

Immediate Policy Concerns:	Init	Date
Patron Confidentiality	___	___
Time Sheets and Time Cards	___	___
Desk Guidelines	___	___
UNO/Circulation student handbooks	___	___
Registering New Patrons:		
Using Odyssey	___	___
Patron Types	___	___
Scanning ID's	___	___
Types of ID accepted	___	___
Reciprocal, Special privileges	___	___
High School	___	___
Proper abbreviations	___	___
Checkouts:		
Date due/Checkout periods	___	___
Reserve Checkouts	___	___
Check Contents	___	___
Item Quantity Limitations	___	___
Desensitizer	___	___
Security Gate	___	___
Gate Log	___	___
"At Desk" Messages	___	___
Manual Checkouts	___	___
Inter-Library Loan	___	___
FLA checkouts	___	___
Checkins:		
Check Contents	___	___
Watching the screen	___	___
Inter-Library Loans	___	___

Checkins *(cont'd.):*	Init	Date
Messages	___	___
Double Discharge	___	___
Sensitizing	___	___
Sorting	___	___
Mending/Targeting	___	___
Materials from other Libraries	___	___
Cash Register Procedures:		
Bad Check list	___	___
Change	___	___
Inter-campus charge	___	___
Copy Cards/ID	___	___
Item sales	___	___
Community User	___	___
Library Friends	___	___
Transparencies	___	___
Laser Print cards	___	___
Mistakes	___	___
Telephone Etiquette:		
Attitude	___	___
Answering	___	___
Asking questions	___	___
Transferring calls	___	___
Know when to say "when"	___	___
Study Rooms:		
Faculty	___	___
Booking system for students	___	___
Keys	___	___

(reprinted with permission of document's creator, Matt Rohde)

Figure 6-3. Training Checklist

Use a checklist to keep track of where each new hire is in his or her training.

Training new staff is exhausting. How can I make this easier?

Enlist others—full-time staff, veteran student staff, even other departments—in the training process. You will be less exhausted and the student being trained will have a richer training experience.

employment eligibility requirements, and emergency procedures (Russell, 1995: 96–97, 99–105). In short, it should include any information to which a student assistant may wish to refer during the course of his or her training or employment. Several student assistant handbooks are reproduced in the sources at the end of this book.

Creating a training manual helps you to train in the most efficient and organized way possible. The training manual should include the goals of the department as well as step-by-step instructions for every task a student will be asked to do. While a training manual is no substitute for hands on active training, it is a valuable reinforcement of important job concepts. Practically speaking, it will also provide you, the trainer, with a much-needed break while training, as you ask the student to review the manual at his or her own pace. This manual will be valuable for the student to refer back to when necessary. Veteran student workers can participate in the creation of various sections of the training manual. Simply ask a student to document all of the steps he or she takes to complete a given task. As the supervisor, you can then edit the various documents that veteran students provide for completeness, appropriateness, and singleness of voice.

1. Train them thoroughly
2. Orient them to their new workplace
3. Clearly define your expectations, regarding both work and conduct

Figure 6-4. Teaching a Student Assistant How to Work

UTILIZE DIFFERENT TRAINERS FOR MAXIMUM COMPREHENSION

Ask current desk staff for a list of the top 10 questions they receive, and provide a list of these questions, with answers, to student assistants.

People respond differently to different communication styles. New student hires may respond better to training provided by other students; hence, veteran students should not be overlooked as a valuable resource in training. A full-time staff member within your unit may also be an appropriate trainer, provided that union guidelines do not dictate otherwise. The training manual can help you to explain to the trainer, be that a student or full-time staff member, exactly what task or responsibility you would like him or her to go over with a new hire. Training provided by several different people is especially useful for Millennial Generation student workers, who do not expect to learn everything from one person and are used to learning from peers (Howe and Strauss, 2000: 155–156). As the supervisor you are ultimately responsible for making sure that new hires are trained properly, so make sure you select your trainers appropriately, and provide them with clear directions on what you'd like them to cover with new hires. You will also want to recap the training the student has received, using the training checklist, to be sure that your designated trainers have clearly communicated everything that the student needs to know on a given topic.

USE THE "SHOW AND TELL" METHOD TO FACILITATE THE PROCESS

When training a student, make sure to show him or her how to do the task at hand, and explain the context for what they will be doing. People tend to retain what they are taught if they are given a context of why various steps are important. For example, to explain the importance of shelving accuracy, tell the trainee that a mis-shelved book is as good as lost. If explaining reliability to a weekend circulation worker, come right out and say that if he or she doesn't turn up for work, it will result in long lines for library patrons. If the student is responsible for staffing the department in the absence of full-time staff, tell him or her that the department will not open if they are late or absent. Reinforce your explanations with the numbers of patrons who rely on library services. Once you have explained how to do the task, observe the trainees performing the task while you explain the steps for them. It is important to let them do whatever it is you are teaching them, be that searching a database, sitting at a keyboard, checking out a book, or wrapping material for shipment because doing the task while you are watching will help to reinforce the proper procedure. Finally, watch them perform the task without reminding them of the steps. Keep an eye out that they do it correctly a few times. This is known as the "show and tell method." The three steps are:

1. The trainer shows the student what to do while simultaneously describing what it is they are doing.

2. The student performs the task, while the trainer describes the steps, providing prompts when necessary.

3. The student performs the tasks while describing what he or she is doing, so the trainer is aware that the student knows what to do.

Be sure to check back often at short time intervals to answer any questions and provide corrective action needed so that bad habits are not formed early on. Mixing in library tours, computer-assisted instruction, and discussions with hands-on work can help students to learn fully their new jobs (Baird, 2003: 23).

> **I find that even the best student workers often fumble on some tasks. How can I avoid that?**
>
> Sometimes, all that is required to help people to understand a task is a little context—why you do it, what's important about it, etc. Also, take a look at the job. Is there a task or responsibility that doesn't fit in, or that otherwise makes the job have too wide a scope? Narrowing the scope can increase student success. After all, students rarely work more than 20 hours per week.

Managers' Roundtable Discussion

Question: What three tips would you offer to facilitate training?

Scott: (1) Have written policies and procedures; (2) Pair new hires up with full-time staff or more experienced students until they feel comfortable with the work; (3) Encourage new hires to ask questions whenever they don't understand something.

Werner: (1) Be consistent and provide everyone with the same training; (2) Provide written instructions or manuals for future reference. This also allows students to concentrate more on what you are saying rather than taking notes; (3) Describe what the end result should be, which helps to give context to various steps in the process.

Bonnie: (1) Start training immediately after hiring them with the most essential information; (2) Provide a written manual; (3) Schedule a new worker with an experienced worker for two weeks.

Conni: (1) Set up a training check list; (2) Give training plenty of time; (3) Let current student assistants train the new ones (this saves you time and helps them to get to know each other, plus it builds the trainer's self-esteem and skills).

Michael: A concise procedures manual, in place and updated regularly, is essential. It's also helpful to have new hires shadow a full-time staff member or supervisor initially as they learn departmental procedures. Students can also help each other with training.

Gary: (1) Bring veteran student assistants into the planning; (2) Browse web sites with new technology discussions (boingboing.net, digg.com, slashdot.org, etc.); (3) Don't forget to train on hardware. New computers have so many new toys built into them that people overlook the opportunity to train on equipment.

Nick: (1) Take the time to explain things thoroughly; (2) Follow a standard training procedure (e.g., written procedures/checklists) but be flexible with this because some students learn at a different pace; (3) Follow up regularly with the student and other staff who work with the student to determine if further training is needed.

Scott Hanscom, Johns Hopkins University
Werner Haun, Library of Congress
Bonnie Hines, Louisiana State University of Alexandria
Conni Kitten, Texas Tech University Libraries

Michael Miller, Queens College—City University of New York
Gary Ploski, Sarah Lawrence College
Nick Rizzo, University of British Columbia

USING ORIENTATION TO ESTABLISH EXPECTATIONS

> Be aware that something as simple as introducing a new hire to other staff can help everyone feel more comfortable.

Orientation is training on the things that help workers feel comfortable in their new job and includes topics as broad as the library's mission statement and as narrow as the location of the nearest restroom. The goal of a successful orientation is to show students how they fit into the larger library picture, and to help them feel that they belong. Failure to create a sense of belonging for a new employee can cause enough discomfort to make him or her think seriously about quitting the job. Orientation should cover:

Where is the bathroom?

Where do I leave my stuff?

How do breaks work?

How do I report hours?

How do I get paid?

What is everyone's name?

What do people prefer to be called?

What is acceptable behavior?

What is unacceptable behavior?

How do I handle safety/security issues?

How do I handle confidentiality issues?

What is the dress code?

How do I use the phone?

> **Even though I'm careful who I hire and train thoroughly, I still have high turnover. What am I doing wrong?**
>
> Sounds like you need to improve your orientation program. Students who have discomfort about their job are unlikely to stay, and not providing proper orientation can make people feel uncomfortable.

The library where you work may already have an established orientation program. If that is the case at your institution, become familiar with what is covered and any necessary specifics to your own departmental orientation program. If your library does not have an orientation program and you need to start one from scratch, talk to current employees to find out what their current job stresses are (often knowledge gaps lead to stress) and what they wished they had known during their first few weeks on the job. Orientation should also provide an understanding of libraries and basic service concepts, such as the organization of materials, conservation issues, and confidentiality. While it might be tempting to assume that every college-bound student has this understanding, it would be a mistake to make that assumption (Baird, 2003: 13). During a new hire's orientation provide him or her with a tour of the office area and introductions to everyone in the area in which he or she will be working, as well as members of library administration. While it may not be possible to introduce every student assistant to the library director, you should at least tell new student hires the names of library and university senior administrators and show photos of them if at all possible. New workers should be shown where to leave their belongings, where the bathroom is, how breaks work, how they report hours, and how they get paid. That's only the tip of the iceberg. Any other information specific to your institution or department should be included in the orientation process.

> Since orientation includes the "big picture" of library services and the physical layout of the library, much of what you'll need to include in student assistant orientation is probably already on your library's website. An appropriate orientation "short cut" may be to ask new student hires to spend some time going over the library website, and taking the various library tutorials which may be posted there (Slagell and Langendorfer, 2003: 281).

Your new hires may have never had a job before so it is as much your job to teach them how to work (i.e., how to conduct themselves in the workplace) as it is your job to teach them how to do the work they were hired to do. You will need to communicate job expectations to them, which will include the amount of work you expect them to complete as well as conduct and performance expectations. Students will need to be clearly told if talking, headphones, cell phone calls, food or beverages are or are

> **Some of my more overcommitted students are constantly trying to rearrange their work schedules to fit with their other extracurricular activities. How can I impress upon them the importance of work time?**
>
> If the schedule changing is disruptive to your own or the department's productivity, you may wish to make a policy that any student who can't make his or her previously agreed upon shift must find a substitute.

not allowed in the immediate work area. Similarly, any office dress code, even if it is simply a definition of appropriate work attire, will need to be explained. Attendance expectations, such as phoning a supervisor when they are too ill to report for work, may seem obvious to you, but are completely new concepts for someone who has never had a job before. It's always best to err on the side of caution where workplace expectations are concerned and articulate your expectations often.

THE UPSIDE AND DOWNSIDE OF "SIGN-OFF" FORMS

Another way to be sure student assistants understand conduct expectations is to ask them to initial a form that says that they have read and understood what is included in their training manual or handbook (as shown in Figure 6-4). Although a common practice at many college and university libraries, you should have your manager, institutional legal counsel, or Human Resources officer approve any contract-like document you prepare for use with any staff.

OFFICE RULES

1. **You are expected to adhere to the schedule which you agreed upon at the start of the semester.**

This cannot be stressed enough. Our department cannot function without you. If you know you will not be in, you must get a sub.

Once your schedule is set, valid excuses for missing work are limited to illness, emergencies, or final exams which happen to be scheduled during your working hours. Homework assignments, studying, or social engagements are NOT valid reasons for missing work; time for these activities should have been figured into your schedule at the beginning of the semester.

Think! Plan ahead! We recognize that your job is not the center of your life here at Anytown College, but your job here is an important responsibility, and we are counting on you.

If you do have difficulty keeping to your schedule, it is possible to work out an adjustment with Jack. Absences, tardiness, or excessive requests for schedule changes are disruptive to the office and can be grounds for dismissal.

2. **Call the ILL office if you cannot work because of illness.**

Please let us know as soon as possible (123-555-1234 to leave a message). Stay home. Feel better.

It is a very serious infraction to call in sick if you are not ill, and then use the time to study or for personal business.

3. **Be on time arriving at work and returning from breaks or lunch periods.**

Call the office if you are running late. Repeated tardiness cannot be tolerated. In most cases, you will not be allowed to make up hours lost through being late.

You are entitled to a 15-minute paid break if you work 3.5 hours in a shift. You MUST take a 30-minute unpaid lunch break if you work more than a 5-hour shift. Please take your break out of the office. Come back rested, well-fed, and ready to work. Please do not count on work time to eat your lunch or snack.

Figure 6-5. Office Rules Document

4. **Office equipment is for business use only.**

Keep the number of personal calls that you make or receive to a strict minimum. Please turn your cell phone off while you are working. We have a limited number of computers, so please don't expect to use office computers for personal use at any time, even if you are not scheduled to work. Also, discourage friends from dropping by the office while you are working.

5. **The Office Dress Code is pretty casual—but remember that while at work you are representing the University and should make a positive impression.**

6. **Food will not be allowed in the office. Covered sodas, coffee, etc., are okay—AS LONG AS YOU ARE OUT OF SIGHT OF THE DOOR AND NOT HANDLING BOOKS OR PERIODICALS.**

Food in the office is undesirable for two reasons: First, if food gets on books or periodicals it damages the paper and attracts insects and other creatures which think of printed matter as something good to eat. Second, it looks unprofessional to patrons who come to the door if they see us eating in the office. Patrons are not allowed to bring food into the building, and they will resent it if they see us munching while on duty.

7. **Your time sheet must be properly filled out and signed if you expect to be paid on time.**

You will be given clear instructions on how to correctly fill out your time sheet, and plenty of advance warning before it is due each pay period. It is a good idea to fill in the hours worked each day as you leave. Be accurate. Make sure your time sheet reflects the hours you actually worked.

8. **Headphones are usually permissible on the job.**

As long as no one else can hear the music, people can still get your attention, you are not watching the door, and it does not distract you from the task at hand. As long as you do not drive others crazy by dancing or singing to yourself.

9. **Ask questions of the full-time staff.**

Talk to us. If there is anything that is not clear—procedures, rules, what's expected of you, where you should go for help, anything—please ask. We will all be working very closely together, and each person's performance affects the work of everyone else in the office. This will only fly if we're all on the same page!

Please sign and date this form to show that you have read and understood all of the above.

Name _____   Date _____

Figure 6-5. Office Rules Document *(Continued)*

THE ORIENTATION CHECKLIST

An orientation checklist can be an effective tool for ensuring all relevant orientation is told to and understood by your new student hires. Similar to the training checklist, the orientation checklist is a comprehensive list of all work- and library-related issues student employees need to know. The line between training and orientation may be difficult to define clearly. Don't worry if you don't know or if you are not sure if your library's Patriot Act Policy should be categorized as training or orientation. The important thing is to make sure students have been exposed to both training and orientation concepts and it is perfectly acceptable to present both categories in a unified document.

Schedule:	Init	Date
Student Schedule	___	___
When you are ill	___	___
Appropriate Reasons for missing work	___	___
Time sheets	___	___
Breaks	___	___
Expectations:	Init	Date
What to do if you don't understand something	___	___
What to do if you don't know what to do next	___	___
What to wear	___	___
Cell phone policy for staff	___	___
Food and drink policy for staff	___	___
Getting Around:	Init	Date
Names	___	___
Organization Chart	___	___
Tour	___	___
Rest Rooms	___	___
Top 10 directional questions	___	___
How to use phone	___	___
The Library:	Init	Date
Mission	___	___
Service Philosophy	___	___

Figure 6-6. Orientation Checklist

My student workers are unfamiliar with many of the library's resources. Should I take time out to ensure that they understand how the system works, even if it means explaining things beyond their job responsibility?

Providing a context for what someone does is really helpful for understanding the importance of the task. But, you must strike a balance between that and providing too much information. Also, if a student is working with the public, and likely to be asked about things in other departments, he or she should certainly have an understanding of the library as a complete system.

DEALING WITH UNIQUE TRAINING ISSUES

At each institution there are special issues that need to be conveyed to staff at all levels, including student assistants. It's important for each supervisor to identify the issues that student workers need to know and incorporate them into the training and orientation process. For instance, what do student workers in your department need to know about confidentiality? The Patriot Act? Patron complaints? Computer or other equipment-use policies? Who is there for backup if a problem arises? If students supervise other students, they will need to be trained how to be effective supervisors. If students work with the public, they will need to be trained in customer service expectations. Any specialized knowledge needs should be covered in training and included in training documents.

KNOW LIBRARY POLICIES THOROUGHLY

All public service staff need to understand library policies in order to explain them to library users. Staff, including student staff, should be familiar with the library's web site, and have appropriate handouts, pamphlets, and pathfinders ready to give to users. All student assistants should be trained on your library's confidentiality policy or any other policy that may be governed by federal or state legislation.

> To be sure that students working with the public have the information they need, teach them to ask clarifying questions.

TRAINING TO TEACH SPECIFIC SKILLS

ANSWER QUESTIONS

Students working with the public need to be trained on how to answer questions. Users don't know which library staff are there to answer which questions and will ask their questions of whomever they feel comfortable approaching—frequently that is a student assistant. Student assistants must be trained how to answer questions, which involves asking one or two clarifying questions in order to be sure they are giving users the information they need. Staff working at the circulation, reserve, or information desks are likely to be asked questions that have to do with other areas of the library. Any student worker in the public eye should know the answer at least to the common questions public service workers receive, even if the questions don't relate to the department in which the student works.

Anyone who has worked in reference knows that the answer to the first question that a patron asks is not always exactly what he or she is looking for. Therefore, the primary objective of staff is to figure out what users need, and either provide it to them, or refer them to someone who can (Jennerich and Jennerich, 1997: 54). Users sometimes disguise true questions as directional questions. For example, they may ask, "Where are the government documents?" The straight answer to the question asked might be, "the second floor," but in order to help the user, he or she should really be referred to the government documents librarian (Jennerich and Jennerich, 1997: 51). Students working in public service can benefit from some basic reference interview training—even if it is just asking one clarifying question—as they often need to clarify even basic questions before they can assist users. For example, if a user asks where he or she can print something out, the answer may differ significantly depending on what needs to be printed out. If a user needs to print from the Internet, he or she can do that in the reference room, but if he or she needs to print a paper, it must be done in the 3rd floor computer lab, for example. Student workers should be trained on how to zero in on the questions that users ask so they can answer them properly (Halsted and Neely, 1990: 63; Jennerich and Jennerich, 1997: 54).

In their book on reference interviewing, Elaine and Edward Jennerich write that the reference interview includes both nonverbal and verbal elements. The nonverbal skills of the reference interview are eye contact, posture, facial expression, and tone of voice. All of these elements contribute to the specific demeanor of the library employee and help to add up to a positive service experience for the user. The verbal skills of the reference interview include remembering the question asked, avoiding a premature diagnosis, asking open-ended questions, paraphrasing the information need, and closing the interview (1997: 11). The best way to train on the reference interview is by simulating questions and role playing responses. During training, staff should be reminded that the most important behaviors in a reference interview include making eye contact with the user, having a positive and appropriate facial expression, keeping a welcoming tone of voice, and remembering the details of the user's question (p. 43). Any student working with the public should be told that it is acceptable to tell a patron they don't know the answer to the question, provided that they refer the patron to someone who can help them (p. 41).

SERVE PATRONS

> Remind students in all departments that they are at work to help library users.

Any student working at a public service desk should be told explicitly that patrons come first, and should be well indoctrinated to the importance of providing good quality customer service. When providing directions to users, staff should be instructed to keep them as simple as possible, and to write them down, if it is helpful to the patron (Jennerich and Jennerich, 1997: 51). When assisting patrons, student assistants should always look interested in what the patron is saying, and not interrupt the patron by providing the answer before he or she is finished asking the question. One of the most globally notable luminaries in the field of library and information science, S. R. Ranganathan, put forth five laws of libraries that shape our thinking when it comes to patron service. They unify all areas of the library, and put the patron first. Ranganathan's laws guide library managers to success. They are:

1. Books are for use—The primary function of library staff is not to safeguard library materials from the potentially malicious hands of patrons; on the contrary, our job is to facilitate use.
2. Books are for all—Everyone in the community is entitled to use the library: to facilitate that, library staff should understand their user community.

3. Every book has its reader—Even the most obscure material is useful to someone, and, as library staff, we are obligated to ensure that people find the information they need at the library.

4. Save the time of the reader—We should provide excellent service and continually improve management to ensure that programs and services are delivered to best serve our patrons.

5. The Library is a growing organism—Libraries will continue to change to meet the changing needs of the patrons they serve.

Ranganathan's five laws provide useful talking points as you train staff on customer service issues.

HANDLE COMPLAINTS

As a supervisor, you should seriously consider if you want student assistants to handle complaints about library service. Handling complaints is difficult, and if not handled well, complaints can easily escalate, resulting in increased frustration for library staff and users. However, if you rely on student assistants to keep service desks open when little or no full-time staff is available, student assistants will not be able to avoid listening to library complaints. If you want students to handle complaints in a way that helps users feel heard and gathers valuable information for you to improve services, you will need to train them to do it properly.

When patrons complain, they want a variety of responses from library staff. The Jennerichs quote Rebecca Morgan's *Calming Down Upset Customers* on this topic, listing the following five needs patrons have when making complaints (p. 23):

1. To Be Taken Seriously—Library staff should not act in any way dismissive of the complaint. It can be helpful for staff to respond to complaints by saying, "We take service complaints really seriously here, and I know my boss will want to hear about this. Can I give you his e-mail address so that you can tell him what happened?"

2. To Be Treated with Respect—Again, acting dismissive or in any way suggesting that the patron invited the negative situation on himself can escalate the situation. Staff should genuinely "turn up" the respect they give whenever a patron makes a complaint.

3. To Get Immediate Action—This may be difficult to provide if student assistants are working without full-time

---

We receive frequent complaints that our student assistants are rude. How can we improve that?

Establish some standards for patron interaction. For example, you may want to require that students working at the circulation desk say, "Hi, may I help you?" instead of saying, "Next." Remind staff that library users often ask us questions that we think are silly, because we know a lot about the library. Stress that it's the silliest, most annoying questions that should not elicit an annoyed response from us. Observe the behavior in public areas to see what specifically, the problem is. It could be that there is only one person who needs some improvement.

supervision on a night or weekend. But, empowering student workers to make exceptions in the name of customer service can be really helpful. If that is not possible, simply tell the patron, "If I were in your position I would want immediate action, but unfortunately the person who can authorize that is not here right now. I can certainly ask them to get in touch with you first thing tomorrow morning."

4. To Ensure the Problem Never Happens Again—Make sure all student workers understand that the library welcomes complaints, since they help us to make and prioritize service improvements. Help staff to genuinely convey this information to patrons.

5. To Be Listened To—Patrons almost always just want to be sure they were heard. Students should understand that they should let the patron make the complaint without interrupting. If the patron is making a loud scene, they can invite the patron into the back area to "discuss the problem" if possible. Staff should be trained to listen for what the real complaint is, employ active listening techniques like paraphrasing, and acknowledge the patron's feelings.

Clearly define the student assistant's role in dealing with user complaints, and ensure that both you and the student assistant agree on that role. Because handling a patron complaint is a risky, high-stakes endeavor, any staff charged with this responsibility should be given ample training and practice in a controlled environment.

SUPERVISE OTHER STUDENTS

Any student who supervises other students will need some guidelines to be sure that they are carrying out this supervision in a way that is acceptable to you, the person in charge. Clearly explain to them what your expectations are on productivity, conduct, and how they are to treat the students they supervise. It is important to have clear documentation for them to follow and tools such as the training checklist and training manual will ensure that they follow your wishes when conducting training, for example. Other documentation can keep their supervisory actions in line with your expectations.

The role of student supervisors should be clearly explained to them. Are they there to simply train new students, or does their role extend to the more complex patron interactions? If they are to deal with more complex problems, be sure to provide training on how you would like those issues addressed.

Someone is doing something wrong. How can I figure out who?

Unless the "something wrong" is a serious, firable offense, the best thing to do is to have a short corrective conversation with everyone. Write down everyone's name on a piece of paper, and go through the list of people until everyone has been retrained in the correct way to do whatever wasn't being done properly.

CONCLUSION

Preparing documentation for training, in the form of training and orientation toolkits makes the training process easier, since it ensures that you will thoroughly train your new student assistants without having to plan the training each and every time you train. During training, keep in mind that you may need to teach your new student assistants about workplace expectations, including acceptable workplace behavior, since they may not have held jobs before. Throughout the training process, testing can help you to know how effective the training has been. Orientation includes opportunities to talk about your expectations as well as the employee's expectations, teach them about the workplace, and meet key people. Prepare all aspects of training, including any specialized training that new student assistants will need, and keep your training tools together in a pre-formed "toolkit" that is ready to put into action at any time.

EXERCISES

EXERCISE 6-1: CREATING A TRAINING CHECKLIST

Write down the major areas of responsibility for the job vacancy. These are the items that the student worker will deal with in a very general way. For example, a circulation worker might handle

1. Registering new patrons
2. Check out
3. Check in
4. Cash register
5. Answering questions (especially over the phone)
6. Reserving study rooms

Once you have determined the major areas of responsibility, write down the subtopics under each major area. For instance, under "registering new patrons" a circulation student worker may need to know:

a. How to use Odyssey
b. Patron categories
c. How to scan IDs

d. Types of ID accepted

e. Reciprocal arrangements or other special privileges

f. Policy for local high school students

g. Acceptable abbreviations used in the system

EXERCISE 6-2: CREATING AN ORIENTATION CHECKLIST

Write down everything a student assistant needs to know in order to be happy working in your area. This might include:

- breaks
- policies
- where supplies are kept
- behavior that's allowed and not allowed
- everyone's name
- answers to frequently asked questions

To determine what to include in your orientation checklist, ask current employees what they need to know or needed to know when they first started in the department. Use this checklist with all employees.

EXERCISE 6-3: RANGANATHAN-GUIDED DISCUSSION

At the next staff meeting, introduce Ranganathan's five Laws of Library Service to departmental staff:

1. Books are for use—The primary function of library staff is not to safeguard library materials from the potentially malicious hands of patrons. On the contrary, our job is to facilitate use.

2. Books are for all—Everyone in the community is entitled to use the library. To facilitate that, library staff should understand their community.

3. Every book has its reader—Even the most obscure material is useful to someone, and, as library staff, we are obligated to ensure that people find the information they need at the library.

4. Save the time of the reader—We should provide excellent service and continually improve management to ensure that programs and services are delivered to best serve our patrons.

5. The library is a growing organism—Libraries will continue to change to meet the changing needs of the patrons they serve.

How might we use these five laws to improve patron experiences at the library?

REFERENCES

Baird, Lynne N. "Student Employees in Academic Libraries: Training for Work, Educating for Life." *PNLA Quarterly* 67, 2 (Winter 2003): 13, 23.

Bortles, Elaine, and Alex Toth. "'I'll take Circulation Policies for 100, Alex' Or, Fostering the Team-Based Approach Among Library Student Assistants." *PNLA Quarterly* 67, 4 (Summer 2003): 14, 20.

Epstein, Carmen. "Using Blackboard for Training and Communicating with Student Employees." *College and Undergraduate Libraries* 10, 1 (2003): 21–25.

Fuller, F. Jay. "Employing Library Student Assistants as Student Supervisors." *College and Research Libraries News* 9 (October 1990): 855–857.

Halsted, Deborah, and Dana Neely. "The Importance of the Library Technician." *Library Journal* (March 1, 1990): 62–63.

Henning, M. M. "Expanding the Role of the Student Desk Assistant in the Electronic Environment." *College and Undergraduate Libraries* 7, 1 (2000): 11–24.

Howe, Neil, and William Strauss. *Millennials Rising: The Next Great Generation*. New York: Vintage Books, 2000.

Jennerich, Elaine, and Edward Jennerich. *Reference Interview as Creative Art*, 2nd Edition. Englewood, CO: Libraries Unlimited, 1997.

Kaye, Beverly L., and Sharon Jordan-Evans. "New Hires: Getting the Right Fit." *Credit Union Executive Journal* 41, 2 (March/April 2001): 32–34.

Nagel, Mary, and Jeanne Malloy. "In Praise of Students as Supervisors." *College and Research Libraries News* 9 (October 1991): 577–578.

Patterson, Maureen. "Overcoming the Hiring Crunch: Tests Deliver Informed Choices." *Employment Relations Today* 27, 3 (Autumn 2000): 77.

Rubin, Richard. *Foundations of Library and Information Science*. New York: Neal-Schuman, 1997.

Russell, Thyra K. "Student Employment Manuals." *Journal of Library Administration* 21, 3/4 (1995): 95–108.

Slagell, Jeff, and Jeanne Langendorfer. "Don't Tread on Me: The Art of Supervising Student Assistants." *The Serials Librarian* 44 (2003): 279–284.

7 KEEPING PERFORMANCE HIGH AND TURNOVER LOW

WHY INVEST IN PERFORMANCE?

Improving student worker morale and job performance is essential to keeping your department running at its best. By maintaining high job satisfaction, you keep performance high and ensure that your department is functioning as efficiently as possible. Furthermore, by building morale you can avoid the continued patron complaints and other customer service problems that are unavoidable when staff is suffering from burnout (Halsted and Neely, 1990: 63). It is a lucky coincidence that morale and performance feed off of one another. Morale is what good performance ultimately comes down to. Keep your student workers happy and they will make you happy. By providing regular feedback on job performance you can take corrective action while problems are still small. By using coaching strategies you can solve performance problems without decreasing morale. As a leader your own motivation and morale at work also affects everyone in your department, so use that powerful tool if morale seems low in your area. Staying engaged and motivated yourself is often the most effective way to motivate others.

> Call around campus to get an idea of the pay scale of various jobs.

STRATEGIES TO KEEP STUDENTS PERFORMING WELL AND RETAIN WELL-PERFORMING STUDENTS

Here's some good news for busy managers: there is one key factor that leads to both good performance and low turnover. Focus on that factor and you will be sure to improve staff work performance while you decrease turnover. What is that magic factor? *Morale*. Here are five things you can do to improve and maintain staff morale.

Our library pays pretty pitifully. How can I keep student workers motivated?

Be sure to provide them with interesting work in an environment where they are happy and comfortable. When it comes to motivation, feelings of contribution and belonging are much better motivators than money.

1. Pay properly
2. Reward
3. Encourage longevity
4. Build the team
5. Develop through mentoring and coaching

PAY PROPERLY

> I can charge a man's battery and then recharge it and recharge it again. But it is only when he has his own generator that we can talk about motivation. He then needs no outside stimulation. He *wants* to do it.
> —Frederick Herzberg, "One More Time," 1996

Most people think that pay is the ultimate motivator and that people work hard because they are motivated by their paycheck. However, experts who study human behavior and motivation believe that this is not the case. They agree that money has little to do with motivation, except when pay is so low that staff can't afford the basic necessities and then it is the lack of money that is functioning as a demotivator. As long as you are paying a student worker enough to meet his or her basic needs, doubling his or her wage would not make the student any more motivated to do a good job. While the lack of money (not getting paid enough to meet one's basic needs) can certainly be a demotivator, money in and of itself is not really a strong motivator. People are much more likely to be motivated by recognition rewards and by the feeling of belonging that comes from team building. Padilla and Patterson discuss the importance of using Hoopla (as described in Thomas J. Peters and Robert H. Waterman's *In Search of Excellence*), the excitement and celebration surrounding meeting all types of goals and milestones, in keeping staff motivated. Keeping jobs interesting, allowing for flexible scheduling, and ensuring continual learning are all ways to keep employees engaged in their jobs, and these factors work much better than monetary rewards (Padilla and Patterson, 1992: 29).

While pay may not create motivation among your staff, pay is certainly related to retention when you consider simple market economics. Let's say that I'm a student worker. I work for minimum wage at the library exit checking bags. The job is kind of boring, but very low stress and although there is no guarantee I can get homework done on the job, occasionally it is slow enough that I can do some of my work. I'm not unhappy with my job, but if my roommate tells me that I can get a job at the gym, loaning equipment to users (a comparable job in that I'm fairly regularly interrupted, but it's low stress, and I might be able to get some of my homework done) for an additional $2 per hour, why wouldn't I change jobs? If I can increase the hourly wage I earn by a couple of dollars by changing jobs, I'll probably do it unless there are other factors keeping me at my library job. Well, maybe occasionally at the library I am assigned to an interesting project? Maybe my boss made cupcakes for my birthday? Maybe he or she listened to my suggestions? A feeling of belonging at work can compete with additional monetary compensation. If you are unable to pay as much as other campus or local jobs think about other non-monetary rewards you can offer to make sure your student assistants have a reason to stay.

REWARD SMARTLY

Simply saying "thank you" goes a long way. Rewards do not need to be extravagant. In fact, they simply need to be SMART.

Specific—Tie a reward to a specific action

Meaningful—Match the reward to the person receiving it—what would they want?

Attainable—Reward small achievements

Relevant—Related to the rewardable behavior

Timely—Reward quickly after the rewardable behavior

Rewards can help to promote an employee's self-esteem. Non-monetary gestures, such as publicly recognizing an employee's positive contributions, will nurture a sense of belonging in employees and remind them that their contribution is important (Padilla and Patterson, 1992: 28, 33). One very easy inexpensive way to reward student workers is to ask for their input on potential programs, the library's web site, new signs, etc. Student workers are an at-the-ready focus group (albeit one that is probably biased, being more knowledgeable about the library than the general population of students) for any potential change in the library. By asking their opinions and suggestions, you not only remind them that they are a vital part of the team, but also get information that can help you to better serve your patrons. Students feel valued if you ask their opinions. And, since we largely serve a student population, students' feedback can be important on many issues such as signage, handouts, web pages, among others.

USE JOB LADDERS TO ENCOURAGE LONGEVITY

A Healthy man [sic] is primarily motivated by the needs to develop and actualize his fullest potentialities and capacities.
—Abraham Maslow, "A Theory of
Human Motivation," 1943

Organizing your department so that you have more than one "layer" of student workers can keep your student staff interested in attaining greater responsibility at work. For instance, if you have students supervising students, or simply have some students performing more complex tasks than others, students see that there is room for them to grow in their jobs and something to strive for. Libraries around the country have utilized the "job ladder" technique to great success. In the course of my research, I heard from dozens of library supervisors, all of whom reported increased retention by using various forms of job ladders. Some even report that a job ladder structure for student workers has helped them to fill full-time positions with well-qualified new graduates. Some departments take a formal approach. Virginia Commonwealth University Library's Access Services department has a four-tier system of increasing responsibility and increasing pay. Beginning student workers start at minimum wage, and with each promotion receive a raise of about $1.00 per hour as compensation for increased responsibility. Students at the top tier are responsible for acting as supervisors during evening, late-night, and weekend hours. Many libraries simply have two levels of student worker: standard and supervisor. Generally, the supervisors are involved in training new student hires. Princeton University's Reserve department reported great success with a two-tier system, noting that student workers sometimes feel more comfortable approaching student supervisors with questions than asking full-time staff. These student supervisors are experienced enough to know when to transfer a problem to full-time staff or managers.

Most formal job ladder programs have a few things in common. First, they pay more when the job requires more responsibility, and second, they give student workers something to strive for. Job ladders could be seen as a way of building in merit and longevity increases, even if your institution does not technically provide merit and longevity increases. Setting up a job ladder does not necessarily require additional money. In fact, if you are unable to provide pay raises, you can use the job ladder to keep students engaged, as the Bookstacks department at the University of Chicago's Regenstein Library does. All of the student workers at the Regenstein Library have the same campus job classification, and the library administration does not have the freedom to give pay raises. As a result, the Bookstacks department, responsible for check-in, reshelving, and all aspects of stack maintenance, has developed a creative approach. They have three levels of students: shelving, circulation check-in, and special projects. Student shelvers must have worked at least one quarter before being considered for advancement and should score either perfect or excellent on department quizzes and shelving checks. As students work their way up the job ladder they are given more responsibility and more varied tasks, but no additional money for performing these tasks. When the library at St. Cloud State University in Minnesota, similarly unable to give raises for additional responsibility, experimented with job ladders, it was initially skeptical about a student's interest in accepting increased responsibility without increased

> If you can't pay a competitive wage, make sure your job offers other positive compensation.

pay. To the administration's surprise, seasoned student workers were interested in taking on more responsibility, even without additional pay, showing that students were motivated by factors other than money (Nagel and Molloy, 1991: 577).

Finally, job ladders do not have to be formal. The library at the prestigious Cooper Union architecture and engineering school in New York City does not have a formal ladder, but still uses the concept of job growth quite effectively: the library recruits students for advanced jobs, such as book repair, archive and visual resources assistance, from the student shelver pool. By establishing a culture that promotes from within, Cooper Union has shown student assistants that their contributions are recognized and rewarded.

> **We have a really great student worker that we don't want to lose. What can we do?**
>
> See about creating a student supervisor position, or another student position that has additional responsibility. Hopefully, that job will also have higher pay. If changing job responsibilities and/or a raise is not possible, try to involve the student in more decision making.

> To get started building a job ladder into your student assistant program, ask yourself the following questions (Letarte et al., 2004: 297).
>
> 1. Where do staff fit in the overall library structure?
> 2. Are there discernible levels of difficulty or skill within the work groups?
> 3. What are the education requirements of each level?
> 4. What are the general skills required by all?
> 5. What are the specific skills required at each level?
> 6. What are the criteria for advancement to the next level?
>
> **Figure 7-1. Questions to Ask When Designing a Job Ladder**

California State University, Chico, implemented a modest job ladder program in its stacks department in 1970. Since that time, the program has grown in its number of student supervisors, their duties, and in the number of departments participating. F. Jay Fuller documents the high rates of retention that this program has created in his 1990 article in *College and Research Libraries News* (pp. 855–856). Andy Spackman, the circulation manager at Brigham Young University, credits the success of his busy department with the student job ladder that they established years ago. Andy and his colleagues consider it part of their responsibility to mentor and instill professionalism in the students who work in the department. By offering a number of different levels of student assistant positions, they are able to promote qualified student assistants to jobs with increasing levels of responsibility.

> Remember that it doesn't take money to build a team, it just takes bringing people together around a common goal or purpose.

Managers' Roundtable Discussion

Question: How do you reduce turnover?

Scott: We have very little turnover. I've reduced turnover by keeping the lines of communication open. I get to know the students and am fairly flexible with their schedules. I thank them often for their hard work and make them feel like members of the team.

Werner: Varying assignments and giving additional responsibility, as well as contextualizing their work as it relates to the library, can help in keeping students interested in the position, and therefore may reduce turnover.

Bonnie: By holding them to pretty high standards and still creating a nurturing environment, we don't have a problem with turnover. We value respect. We call our student assistants "reference assistants" and insist that they respect supervisors and staff as well as each other. We don't encourage tattling and don't tolerate any last-minute "can't come to work" calls unless it is a legitimate emergency. We are flexible in scheduling and remember that their college experience is broader than their work in the library. Communication is another important value. We give clear instructions about their duties, and observe them to be sure they understand. We keep everyone in the loop on news—we use an e-mail list for Reference Assistants to alert them to new databases or new assignments that faculty have given to their classes.

Conni: To reduce turnover, hire well, treat your students well, and be consistent.

Michael: I reduce turnover by keeping in close communication with student assistants, being flexible in crunch times, offering extra work during breaks, and offering the potential for increases in status and remuneration.

Gary: I like to have monthly or semesterly gatherings of all of the student assistants, one-on-one meetings with new student assistants during their first semester (to discuss their concerns/likes, etc. and plan out their future interests within ACD), and remind myself that they are students first and employees second.

Nick: I try to be flexible during the year. At certain times, students will have school commitments (e.g., papers, exams). I try to accommodate these things by allowing them to trade shifts with others, changing their schedules, and so on. If you are too rigid and give students no options, they will most likely quit (since school is their first priority) or they will not work up to their capabilities.

Scott Hanscom, Johns Hopkins University
Werner Haun, Library of Congress
Bonnie Hines, Louisiana State University of Alexandria
Conni Kitten, Texas Tech University Libraries

Michael Miller, Queens College—City University of New York
Gary Ploski, Sarah Lawrence College
Nick Rizzo, University of British Columbia

BUILD YOUR STUDENT ASSISTANTS INTO A COHESIVE TEAM

A worker who feels comfortable with his or her surroundings is much more likely to enjoy his or her job and therefore much more likely to stick with it. There are many strategies for team building, but they all have one factor in common: bringing the group together. This can be accomplished both by physically bringing a group together for a special purpose and by creating a common purpose in a less concrete way. One of the easiest ways to bring a group together is by having regular staff meetings. If you can't

Games	Departmental List	Celebrating Milestones
Cake or other goodies	Group Projects	Sharing Statistics
Pizza	Regular Meetings	Clear Goals

Figure 7-2. Team Building Strategies

get the entire group together every time (admittedly, it is difficult to schedule a staff meeting that accommodates all student workers because of class schedules) you can still achieve positive results by having frequent staff meetings even if not everyone can attend every meeting. More informal get-togethers, such as pizza parties or outings, are also beneficial for helping staff get to know each other and building the team. Technology like Blackboard and WebCT can be used to create real-time or asynchronous virtual meetings. Establishing clear goals and providing feedback for everyone regarding department statistics and milestones also helps to build a team by getting everyone behind a common goal. A group office clean-up day can also have the same effect. Use your creativity to find ways to help build your team.

> **How can I create a work environment that students actually enjoy coming to?**
>
> Make sure your expectations are reasonable, be firm but fair and occasionally provide them with treats and goodies!

Creating a student task force or committee is another way to build a sense of belonging among student staff, as well as bringing student workers together from different library departments. The Scott Memorial Library at Pacific University in Forest Grove, Oregon, in the interest of improving communication, training, and morale of student workers, developed a student task force. The task force determined that the library's student assistants primarily wanted a greater understanding of day-to-day library operations and how their work fit into the larger picture of the library mission. They were curious about the functions of library departments other than their own. In an effort to provide an opportunity for this kind of learning in a fun environment, the student task force organized a library quiz night for student assistants. Each team was comprised of students from different library departments, which helped to foster a team spirit across departmental boundaries. Not only was the quiz night a resounding success, but the planning process also proved beneficial for the morale of those students involved (Bortles and Toth, 2003: 14, 20).

MENTOR METHODICALLY

Think for a moment that I have magically transported you to a foreign land. Perhaps the land is here on Earth, or perhaps it is on another planet. The people look different from you, speak a language you have never heard before, and use an unfamiliar alphabet. The terrain looks like nothing you have ever seen and you don't know how to navigate the area. How

> **I overheard a student very confidently giving incorrect information about the library to a patron. How should I go about correcting him?**
>
> As soon as possible after the incident, ask to speak with the student one-on-one. Relay what you heard and tell him the correct information in a non-judgmental way. Provide an opportunity for him to ask questions to be sure that he understands the issue correctly. Thank the student and offer some words of encouragement to maintain his self-esteem.

do you feel? Comfortable? I think not. Adventurous, maybe, but definitely not comfortable. Keep that in mind when you are training student assistants. Because we know our way around our department and library so well, we sometimes forget that the library can be an intimidating place for those who don't know it so well. Continually put yourself in your new hires' shoes to understand what they need to know. Ask them what is unfamiliar and provide a workplace where it is comfortable for them to respond honestly. Providing them with proper training and orientation greatly increases retention.

Training is a constant process, and staff should be given regular reminders about important issues and tested periodically to be sure they understand and know how to follow established procedures (Slagell and Langendorfer, 2003: 282). Employees are never "fully trained," because procedures and services change. Students should be provided with continual training, including periodic tours and information about the location of various departments and services within the library. Check in with students regularly on the types of questions they receive from users or the questions they have about workflow and procedure. Use this information to fight the discomfort of not knowing.

> **Our student workers are all over the map in terms of productivity and quality. What can we do?**
>
> Evaluate all of your student workers. If your department has measurable outputs, obtain quantitative data on student productivity. Let them know how they measure up. If standards for judgment are more subjective, observe student performance before providing evaluations. Use coaching as a way to provide feedback in a non-personal way.

EVALUATING REGULARLY

All staff require feedback about their job performance. Feedback can be in the form of a formal evaluation, or may simply be short, regular counseling sessions in which a supervisor comments on an observed behavior. The more often feedback is given, the more opportunities a student has to improve his or her job performance.

The job description is essential to the evaluation process. After all, how can a student perform well unless he or she knows what is expected? Both supervisor and staff must have a shared, clear understanding of the level of performance that is expected, so be sure to communicate your expectations to your student staff. Monitor performance regularly, and administer evaluations based on established job criteria that are based on observed task performance, not personality (Giesecke, 1992: 21). Students should be evaluated on the following ten criteria (Russell, 1995: 105):

1. Attendance/punctuality
2. Attitude/service
3. Communication
4. Initiative
5. Judgment

6. Observance of policies
7. Productivity and quality of work
8. Responsibility
9. Training of others
10. Working relationships

Be quick about reacting when performance slips. Ignoring a performance problem sends the impression that the performance is acceptable even if it is not. Thus, when you see one of your student assistants talking on his or her mobile phone when that has expressly been communicated as unacceptable workplace conduct, you are obligated to say something. A simple, unapologetic, "Jane, please hang up your phone," is the best way to keep student assistants from assuming that the policy has been relaxed. If there is a problem and someone is not meeting expectations, document the specifics of the issue. Since you may be required to submit documentation centrally or document in a specific way, take notes on the performance problems that you observe, including dates of specific instances of problem behavior and names of witnesses to the behavior, and record any actions you take (Slagell and Langendorfer, 2003: 283). Talk to your boss or the Human Resources department to learn the local procedures for documenting performance problems. The most effective way to deal with low performers is to communicate to them promptly and clearly what is expected and how their current performance differs from the desired performance, and establish a plan for corrective action and set a date in the future to check back in about performance. This is called *coaching*.

Keep in mind that training is a continuous process.

Be consistent in your workplace expectations.

Two of my student workers are angry with each other about something from their personal life, and I fear it may disrupt their work. Should I intervene or leave well enough alone?
If you are noticing it, it's probably already affecting the workplace. Keep your communications with them professional, and focus on the work that is not getting done, or the way the hostility has affected morale in the department. Speak to each student individually, and address behavior and performance problems specifically and objectively.

USING COACHING CONVERSATIONS TO TACKLE CORRECTIVE ACTION

Coaching is a way to take corrective action in a non-personal manner. It's a way to confront the problem, not the individual, and help to improve performance. Coaching means using your enthusiasm, knowledge, and support to help an employee solve a problem that is keeping him or her from optimal performance. As a tool, it is as equally useful when an employee has developed a problem behavior as it is when a non-problematic employee simply could improve an aspect of his or her job performance. The most important part of a coaching conversation is to keep a positive, solution-oriented attitude (Geisecke, 1992: 23). As a supervisor, your role is to facilitate change in the employee's performance, to do everything you can to make it easy for them to improve. Project the attitude that they can change and that you'll do everything you can to help them.

A student with shelving responsibility in the stacks has asked my permission to listen to music on his iPod while working. Should I let him?
Is the student generally a good worker and accurate shelver? You may want to reward him (and similar good shelvers) with the privilege of using their iPods at work. Provided it doesn't interfere with patron service or quality work, an iPod may be a useful tool for keeping your student workers happy during more routine tasks.

Example 1:

Step 1: Present one issue that needs improvement in a specific, future-oriented way.

Supervisor: "Joe, over the past two weeks, you have been late to work 4 times; last Monday and Wednesday you were 15 minutes late and this week you were 20 minutes late on Monday and Wednesday. We need you to be here to open the Reserve desk. Let's talk about how to solve this problem."

Step 2: Diffuse any resistance, learn about the employee's concerns, and agree on problems, causes, and solutions. (Note: This step involves active listening, and may involve a large degree of back and forth with the individual.)

Joe: "What's the big deal? I always stay later when I arrive late."

Supervisor: "I do appreciate that you are conscientious about working a full day, but please understand that I've received some patron complaints about the desk opening late. Let's try to figure out a constructive solution that meets everyone's needs. What has caused this recent lateness? What is it about Mondays and Wednesdays?"

Joe: "I have to bring my daughter to school on Monday and Wednesday mornings. I try to get here as soon as I can, but lately the traffic has been so bad that I can't seem to get here by 8:30."

Supervisor: "This makes me wonder, if you've been bringing your daughter to school since September. Has the traffic just recently gotten worse?"

Joe: "Yes! I think it is because of the road construction on route 50. Everyone seems to be taking the secondary roads, and it really snarls things up."

Supervisor: "That makes sense. Is it possible to drop your daughter off at school earlier?"

Joe: "No, it's really not. She's only 5, and as it is, she's one of the first kids dropped off. I wouldn't want her to wait around the school alone. She's just way too young for that."

Supervisor: "Hmm, since you always stay late on the days that you arrive late, I'm assuming that you don't have a similar time-bound commitment in the evening?"

Joe: "No, her mother picks her up from school."

Supervisor: "One solution might be for you to work 9–6 on Mondays and Wednesdays and keep your regular 8:30–5:30 schedule on Tuesday, Thursday, and Friday, provided I can ask someone else in the department to start a little earlier. This change would be temporary, since road construction on route 50 is scheduled to be complete in two months. Would that work?"

Joe: "That would certainly work for me—do you think anyone would be interested in adjusting their schedule?"

Supervisor: "The day time slots are usually pretty coveted, so I think Bret or Sally might be interested. I'll see what I can do."

Step 3: Build strategies for solution, go over the key issues, and express confidence that the situation can be corrected.

Supervisor: "OK, Joe, I'll see about getting someone else to open the desk on Mondays and Wednesdays until the road work on route 50 is complete in two months. This would have been a lot easier to deal with had you told me about the issue a couple of weeks ago when it first started. Next time, I know you'll come to me with a problem before it becomes critical."

Joe: "I appreciate how accommodating you've been. Yes, I'll definitely work with you on these matters before they grow into big problems."

Figure 7-3. Coaching Conversations

If coaching is new to you, it can be awkward at first. Be sure to prepare your coaching conversation before you begin. If you are coaching someone about a problem behavior, the conversation should follow these five steps:

Example 2:	
Step 1: Present one issue that needs improvement in a specific, future-oriented way. *Supervisor:* "Katie, in examining the departmental statistics, I've noticed that your error rate is higher than I'd like to see, at 22 percent. I was hoping that you and I could talk about some ways we could improve that."	*Katie:* "And, I feel a little stressed out about productivity quotas." *Supervisor:* "OK, I can understand that. Keep in mind, though, that accuracy is much more important than numbers. I think with a little bit of additional training and attention, you can improve your productivity as well as your accuracy."
Step 2: Diffuse any resistance, learn about the employee's concerns, and agree on problems, causes, and solutions. (Note: This step involves active listening, and may involve a large degree of back and forth with the individual.) *Katie:* "What? I had no idea! That can't be right." *Supervisor:* "Please understand that I am not bringing this up to make you feel bad, but rather because I know you can do better, and I'd like to help you. Here's an example of a cataloging copy record that you imported, but it's for the 1995 edition, when the book we have is the 2003 edition." *Katie:* "Oh, I didn't see that." *Supervisor:* "Any thoughts on the causes for such a mistake?" *Katie:* "Well, I'm a little confused about how to navigate around the system." *Supervisor:* "Ok, well, we can get you some more training on that."	***Step 3: Build strategies for solution, go over the key issues, and express confidence that the situation can be corrected.*** *Katie:* "I would like to become an expert. I can't stand feeling like I don't know what I'm doing." *Supervisor:* "OK, well why don't you and I spend an hour or so a few times a week over the next few weeks on navigating the system? In fact, I'd be happy to set up a schedule for us to do that, then we can look at your numbers and monitor your improvement. Jared is also a whiz with the system, so I'll ask him to sit down with you to show you some of his tricks." *Katie:* "That sounds good." *Supervisor:* "One of the reasons I wanted to have this conversation is because you are important to this organization and we want to see you succeed. I think with a little more training, we can be sure that you become an expert copy cataloger."

Figure 7-3. Coaching Conversations *(Continued)*

1. Be specific
2. Be future oriented
3. Agree on a problem and its causes
4. Strategize for improvement
5. Follow through

FOCUS ON A SINGLE, SPECIFIC ISSUE

Bring up a specific issue during a coaching conversation, rather than a vague problem or laundry list of unrelated problem behaviors. Say, "You were late on Monday, Wednesday and Friday last week" rather than

> When it is necessary to confront an employee on a behavioral problem, prioritize which issues need addressing and counsel the employee on one behavior at a time.

saying, "You seem to have trouble getting to work on time," or, "You have a problem with lateness, a bad attitude, and poor personal hygiene." By presenting one issue in an objective way you show the staff member that it is not a personal attack but rather a problem behavior that needs improvement. By focusing on a single problem you avoid overwhelming the staff member and present the problem as something that can be solved.

ANCHOR THE DESIRED RESOLUTION IN THE FUTURE

Couch the reason why the behavior must change in terms of what is desired in the future. For example, "We need you to be on time in the future so that we can ensure the work gets done. How can we make that happen?" Listen to what the employee has to say, and be prepared to discuss the reasons the employee may provide as explanation for his or her performance issues. These reasons are key to solving the problem—if you know why an employee is late you can figure out what to do to ensure the employee stops coming in late.

Work with the employee to come to a consensus about the reason for the problematic behavior and why it is occurring. Often, simply identifying causes of the behavior can point to a really simple solution. The lateness may be caused by childcare problems, transportation issues, or a schedule change in personal commitments. Once you know what is causing the lateness you and the employee can work together to fix it.

ENCOURAGE EMPLOYEE STRATEGIES

Prompt the employee to suggest ways that he or she could improve the behavior. The solution has a better chance of being successful if the employee thinks of it. Hence, if the employee identifies the cause of lateness as a transportation problem, ask the employee what some alternatives might be to his or her current transporation arrangement. Perhaps the subway has a better schedule than the bus? Perhaps if the employee left five minutes earlier he or she wouldn't get stuck behind the school bus? Prompt the employee to suggest options. Present the issue in terms of what is needed, for example, "We really need someone to be here at 8:45 to open the department—how can we solve this problem?" and wait for a response. Be sure to give plenty of time for the employee to consider the question and be ready to ask stimulating questions if they can't think of an immediate solution.

FOLLOW THROUGH ON SHARED PLANS

Set a date to follow up with the employee. Affirm that you believe in the employee and know that improvement will happen. Remind yourself and the employee that you will work together to solve the problem.

1. Be specific—what is the one issue you wish to bring up?
2. Be future oriented
3. Agree on a problem and its causes
4. Strategize for improvement
5. Follow through

Figure 7-4. Blank Coaching Outline

GUIDELINES FOR HANDLING DISCIPLINE ISSUES

If the problem you are trying to solve relates to conduct, your human resources department or supervisor can provide you with guidelines for handling the situation and keeping written records of what transpired. Your institution probably has a zero tolerance policy for some issues, such as theft, and those conduct problems will probably be addressed with immediate termination. Other conduct problems will be addressed with verbal or written warnings. To prepare for a conversation with an employee whose conduct has been a problem, fully investigate the incident or issue. Gather data (statistics, what you observed, what others observed) to make your case. As in the coaching conversation, it's important to get the employee to agree that there is a problem. These conversations can be nerve-wracking for both supervisor and staff. Give the employee time to digest the information and don't talk non-stop. Explain the consequences of not changing and help the employee find a solution to the problem. Monitor the change, and set a follow-up date for evaluating the employee's progress (Giesecke, 1992: 25).

TERMINATE CONFIDENTLY

One hundred percent retention is not possible. Some would argue that 100 percent retention isn't even desirable (think about some of the long-timers in your workplace who underperform). Termination is never pleasant, but it is a necessary evil of being a supervisor. By thoroughly training staff, and continually coaching them to improve any performance problems that occur, you can keep termination to a minimum. If a student worker is simply not working out and is a low performer in every aspect of the job, one approach is to retrain the person. Often times, when you approach the student and say that you don't think that they were properly trained the first time around, and that you'd like to start the training process over, they simply decide that they don't want to work in that capacity anymore. If you do initiate the retaining process, it will likely improve the student's job performance. If it does not lead to improved performance, then the retraining effort can provide some evidence to back up a termination. Keep documentation on all performance problems in accordance with your local practices. Your boss or human resources officer can tell you what the documentation guidelines are for your organization, but usually they are adding written documentation to an individual's official personnel file. Be familiar with your organization's appeal process for discipline or terminations. Documenting performance issues is essential if a terminated student worker contests the decision to let him or her go.

Sooner or later you will have to let someone go. Keep in mind that it is better to have no student worker than a problem student worker (Slagell and Langendorfer, 2003: 281). Working with your human resources department throughout the coaching and discipline process will ensure that you have enough evidence to make such a decision. Speak to HR or your supervisor about the best way to terminate an employee. Generally, the conversation must be honest, forthright, and direct. Don't forget the pragmatics: escort the student to clean out his or her locker or workspace; collect any ID card or keys issued; rescind any special privileges (for example, special borrowing privileges) extended to the student; and ensure that centralized records reflect the reason for termination.

EXPLORING BASIC THEORIES OF MOTIVATION

While this book is primarily a practical handbook, taking a look at some theories can be really helpful when trying to explore what motivates students working in your department. Remember that people can't "be motivated": they motivate themselves. But you can tap into their own motivation by creating an environment that allows their intrinsic motivation to thrive.

USE MASLOW TO MOTIVATE SPECIFICALLY

Abraham Maslow's often discussed (often simplified) theory of human motivation puts forth the idea that human beings satisfy needs in a particular order. That is to say that some needs are more basic than others and must be satisfied before a person can begin to think about higher, more complex needs. While motivation is only part of what determines behavior, Maslow organized human needs into a hierarchy representing the order in which we seek to meet our needs (Maslow, 1943: 371). Maslow's hierarchy of needs is represented in Figure 7-5.

> **We terminated a student worker who was just terrible—her attendance record was about 50 percent, and when she did come to work, she resisted completing any assignment that was given to her. We provided this student with several warnings (some of them written) and engaged in a coaching process to improve her performance. After she was terminated (none of our extra effort having worked), her mother threatened to sue me for wrongful termination. What can I do?**
>
> Relax. Sounds like you have all the written documentation you need to prove your position. Be sure your boss or HR person knows what has transpired, and has copies of all the documentation. Keep your boss or HR representative in the loop with what transpires. One of the reasons to keep documentation on such issues is to protect yourself in the event someone challenges your decision to terminate an employee.

> Keep a centralized record of any terminations so that your colleagues don't hire the same person and repeat the problem all over again.

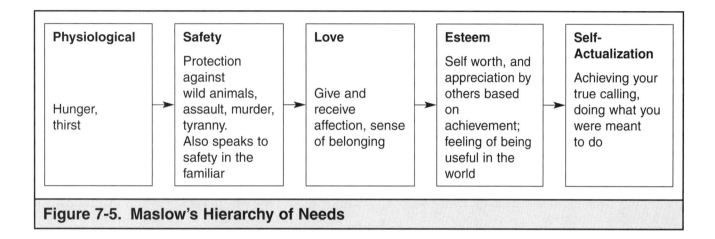

Figure 7-5. Maslow's Hierarchy of Needs

Simplistically speaking, Maslow's theory of human motivation states that people must satisfy needs in a certain order. A person must first address life-threatening issues related to hunger and thirst (in a grand scheme, not just taking a coffee break or eating a snack) before he or she can address other needs, and whichever need a person must address is the one to which he or she gives the greatest importance. In our society, it is rare for an individual not to have his or her basic physiological needs met. Here in the United States, we are not in a state of famine or drought, and while we may colloquially say "I'm starving" right before lunch, it's unlikely that we are actually in any danger of starving to death. Similarly, we are also comparatively safe. While unsafe situations do arise, they are uncommon enough not to be in the forefront of our minds at any given moment, and therefore, Maslow contends that physiological needs and needs for safety do not generally function as motivators for employees (p. 379).

Once a need is satisfied, it ceases to influence behavior. Since most employees' basic physical needs are met and it is rare for students not to have a place to sleep, physiological and safety needs are no longer on their radar screen. They look for higher needs to be met, those further up the hierarchy, like the freedom to do what they wish, express creativity, or the desire to know and understand their workplace (pp. 383–386).

When looking for ways to tap into what motivates employees to perform well at work, think beyond money. Instead, focus on the final three stages in Maslow's hierarchy: Love, Esteem, and Self-Actualization. Team-building activities and mentoring can give a sense of belonging that equates to the "love" stage in Maslow's hierarchy, and providing a reward structure or job ladder fulfills the need for esteem. Very few people reach the stage of Self-Actualization, but those student workers that we occasionally meet, the ones who move on to pursue library degrees or full-time library work, may be exhibiting signs of achieving self-actualization.

Day jobbers:

Individuals working in libraries, particularly those who do not hold degrees in library science, often look at their work in the library as simply a "day job." It is sometimes difficult for librarians, particularly those who are passionate about their profession, to understand that individuals they supervise don't hold their job as a high priority. This is particularly true for student assistants. For them, school comes first. There are particular strategies that you can employ to make this issue much less daunting than it sounds.

A surprising number of people work in the library at every level and do so to support their activities and interests outside of library work. Recently, I asked a class of 15 library staff (mostly librarians and non-MLS library supervisors) how many of them worked in the library as a "day job" to support other pursuits. Fully one-third said they did; most work in the library to support creative endeavors such as acting, painting, or screenwriting (of course, these folks all lived and worked in the New York City area, so my survey was hardly scientific). More than half of my own department of approximately 50 regular employees (not including students) work at the library to support other creative or intellectual pursuits. People accept jobs for a variety of reasons. You may have accepted your job because you are personally rewarded by each and every task inherent in it; it may feed your soul. Or, you may be working at your job until you can make money from your other interests, the interests that feed your soul. The "I work at this library job until I can make money from my interests" sentiment is likely to be the case at most large academic libraries. Remember, this is a perfectly

legitimate reason to work! If you find yourself thinking that the "day jobbers" you work with aren't serious enough or even worse "as serious as I am" about working in the library, it's time for a reality check. Many universities offer tuition-remission benefits to full-time staff, and so even the full-time staff is likely to be students.

Do you need to manage day jobbers differently from managing people for whom library work was their primary pursuit? Since people are motivated by their own terms and needs, it just makes sense to acknowledge the different core reasons that people hold day jobs as opposed to the reasons why people might be fulfilled by library work. There are a number of differences between day jobbers and "primary pursuiters."

Day jobbers are motivated by:

- Deferred Goals: their work is a means to an end, and not an end in and of itself.
- Tangible Benefits: a paycheck or health insurance.
- Daily Efficiency: to make their job easier.

Primary Pursuiters are motivated by:

- Actualized Goals: their genuine primary interest in library work is more likely to be motivated by details of the actual library work.
- Intangible Benefits: an understanding of the details of why we do what we do.
- Daily Efficiency: to make systems work better.

Figure 7-6. Managing "Day Jobbers"

DRAW ON HERZBERG TO MOTIVATE INTRINSICALLY

Frederick Herzberg researched motivational theory through the 1950s and 1960s by investigating on-the-job motivation among engineers and accountants in middle-management positions in Pittsburgh, Pennsylvania (Steuart and Moran, 1998: 278). His theories build on Maslow's but are applied specifically to the workplace. Herzberg and his associates extensively surveyed workers about what they wanted from their jobs, and ultimately concluded that, "the opposite of job satisfaction is not job dissatisfaction, but rather no job satisfaction; and, similarly, the opposite of job dissatisfaction is not job satisfaction, but no job dissatisfaction" (Herzberg, 1968: 56). To illustrate this point, Herzberg notes that if you kick a dog, the dog moves, and if you hold up a dog treat, the dog also moves, but neither situation illustrates any motivation on the part of the dog. In fact, in both examples, the person (either kicking or offering a treat) is the one who is motivated (i.e., has the desire) to get the dog to move. The trick is to get the dog to *want* to move. To use a workplace example, a supervisor may yell at an employee who is surly to a patron, or may give a chocolate bar to an employee who treats a patron well, but neither activity helps staff to want to provide good service. Reward systems (the dog treat or the chocolate bar in the examples) are sometimes mistaken for motivation, but they are not motivation (p. 54). Herzberg would call rewarding employees, "positive KITA," where KITA stands for "Kick in the A**." While he is right that rewards for good behavior do not help employees to understand the reason why the good behavior is encouraged, and that rewards may not be sustainable over the long term, they do bring about short-term movement, which is certainly beneficial while you work toward longer-term motivation. True motivation comes from an understanding and acceptance of why certain behaviors are valued.

> **I just started a job where I manage a large group of students. I can tell that morale is low. How do I get started in improving things?**
>
> Sounds like the previous supervisor probably didn't treat them with much respect. Make an appointment to meet with each student, and ask for constructive ways you can improve the department. Listen to their suggestions, and implement as many good ideas as you can. Have a meeting with all of the student staff. Make it a kick-off party for your new way of doing things. Make sure you have some food and drinks, and make the primary purpose getting to know each other. Remember that improving morale is a long-term project, but listening to staff is the first step.

AN INTERESTING JOB IS THE BEST MOTIVATOR

To truly tap into motivation, take a little bit from many different motivational theorists, and filter it through your own experience. Herzberg says that people are motivated by what motivates them, and that not only does motivation differ from person to person, a person's motivation changes depending on his or her circumstances. What's the best way to determine what motivates someone? Ask them.

All major motivational theorists conclude that an interesting job is more of a motivator than material incentives or rewards. It's our challenge to find a way to make all jobs interesting. Even the most routine job has a purpose for being done, so share that with the person doing it. Jobs become more interesting to the people who perform them if they know the context of the task they are performing. Think about ways that routine jobs can be combined with more interesting work. Ask students charged with performing the jobs how they could be improved.

One of the best ways to build morale is to show respect for the people who report to you. Keep them informed of developments in the organization, share positive comments with them about the department that you receive from patrons. When complaints come in, share them, too, but only in the spirit of soliciting feedback for improvement (Halsted and Neely, 1990: 63) Engaging workers at all levels in conversations about service improvement will not only result in improved processes, but will help users to feel more motivated to do well at work. They not only will own the improved processes, but they will have "bonded" with colleagues they have worked with to make the improvements and will therefore have a heightened feeling of belonging in the organization.

The most important action supervisors can take when it comes to plugging into people's motivation is to lead by example. Staying continually engaged on the job and having a fulfilling, balanced life will lead to happiness in all areas, including work. I'm not saying that simply being happy at your job will make those who report to us happy at work, but have you ever worked for someone who was miserable? What a demotivator. Keep your interest and attitude up and it will set a motivated, engaged tone for the entire department.

> Lead by example in morale and work habits.

CONCLUSION

Morale and job performance go hand in hand—good morale leads to good job performance, which leads to feeling good about one's abilities, which leads to good morale. Conversely, low morale leads to poor job performance. Invest in your employees' performance and you will be rewarded with retention. Team building and coaching will help to build morale among the people in your department. Staying motivated yourself is the best way to motivate others.

EXERCISES

EXERCISE 7-1: PAY EQUITY

Call five different campus departments and find out what they pay their
student assistants.

Department	Starting Hourly Wage	Student Assistant Responsibilities

EXERCISE 7-2: MOTIVATION

Think about the student assistants who work in your department. Make some notes regarding what you think motivates them and ask them what motivates them. Note any progress made in motivation over a two-month period.

What you think motivates your student assistants:

What your student assistants say motivates them:

Progress made in motivation over a two-month period:

REFERENCES

Baird, Lynn N. "Student Employees in Academic Libraries: Training for Work, Educating for Life." *PNLA Quarterly* 67, 2 (Winter 2003): 13, 23.

Bortles, Elaine, and Alex Toth. "'I'll take Circulation Policies for 100, Alex' Or, Fostering the Team-Based Approach Among Library Student Assistants." *PNLA Quarterly* 67, 4 (Summer 2003): 14, 20.

Burrows, Janice. "Training Student Workers in Academic Libraries: How and Why?" *Journal of Library Administration* 21, 3/4 (1995): 77–86.

"Deming System of Profound Knowledge." The W. Edwards Deming Institute. September 19, 2005. www.deming.org/theman/teaching.html and www.deming.org/theman/teachings02.html.

Dermody, Melinda, and Susan Schlepper. "Supervising: What They Didn't Teach You in Library School?" *College and Research Libraries News* 65 (June 2004): 306–308, 332.

Fuller, F. Jay. "Employing Library Student Assistants as Supervisors." *College and Research Libraries News* 9 (October 1990): 855–857.

Giesecke, Joan. "Performance Appraisal." In *Practical Help for New Supervisors*. Edited by Joan Giesecke. Chicago: American Library Association, 1992.

Halsted, Deborah, and Dana Neely. "The Importance of the Library Technician." *Library Journal* (March 1, 1990): 62–63.

Herzberg, Frederick. "One More Time: How Do You Motivate Employees?" *Harvard Business Review* 46 (January/February 1968): 53–62.

Jennerich, Elaine, and Edward Jennerich. *Reference Interview as Creative Art*, 2nd Edition. Englewood, CO: Libraries Unlimited, 1997.

Letarte, Karen M., Charles Pennell, and Shirley Hamlett. "Creating Career Paths for Cataloging Support Staff." *In Innovative Redesign and Reorganization of Library Technical Services: Paths for the Future and Case Studies*. Edited by Bradford Lee Eden. Westport, CT: Libraries Unlimited, 2004.

Maslow, Abraham. "A Theory of Human Motivation." *Psychological Review* 50 (July 1943): 370–396.

Nagel, Mary, and Jeanne Molloy. "In Praise of Students as Supervisors." *College and Research Libraries News* 9 (October 1991): 577–578.

Nelson, Bob, and Peter Economy. *Managing for Dummies*. Foster City, CA: IDG Books, 1996.

Padilla, Irene M., and Thomas Patterson. "Rewarding Employees Nonmonetarily." In *Practical Help for New Supervisors*. Edited by Joan Giesecke. Chicago: American Library Association, 1992.

Russell, Thyra K. "Student Employment Manuals." *Journal of Library Administration* 21, 3/4 (1995): 95–108.

Slagell, Jeff, and Jeanne Langendorfer. "Don't Tread on Me: The Art of Supervising Student Assistants." *The Serials Librarian* 44 (2003): 279–284.

Steuart, Robert D., and Barbara B. Moran. *Library and Information Center Management*, 5th ed. Englewood, CO: Libraries Unlimited, 1998.

SOURCES: MANAGING STUDENT ASSISTANTS

A: BIBLIOGRAPHY
B: WEB LINKS TO RECOMMENDED POLICIES AND PROCEDURES
C: SAMPLE STUDENT WORKER HANDBOOK

SOURCE A: BIBLIOGRAPHY

Association of Research Libraries. *ARL Statistics: Interactive Edition.* www.fisher.lib.virginia.edu/arl.

Baird, Lynne N. "Student Employees in Academic Libraries: Training for Work, Educating for Life." *PNLA Quarterly* 67, 2 (Winter 2003): 13, 23.

Baldwin, David A., Frances C. Wilkinson, and Daniel C. Barkley. *Effective Management of Student Employment: Organizing for Student Employment in Academic Libraries.* Englewood, CO: Libraries Unlimited, 2000.

Bortles, Elaine, and Alex Toth. "'I'll take Circulation Policies for 100, Alex' Or, Fostering the Team-Based Approach Among Library Student Assistants." *PNLA Quarterly* 67, 4 (Summer 2003): 14, 20.

Burrows, Janice. "Training Student Workers in Academic Libraries: How and Why?" *Journal of Library Administration* 21, 3/4 (1995): 77–86.

Dawes, Trevor, Kimberly Burke Sweetman, and Catherine Von Elm. *Access Services* (SPEC Kit 290). Washington, DC: Association of Research Libraries, 2005.

DeBard, Michael. "Millennials Coming to College." *New Directions for Student Services* 106 (Summer 2004): 33–45.

"Deming System of Profound Knowledge." The W. Edwards Deming Institute. September 19, 2005. www.deming.org/theman/teaching.html and www.deming.org/theman/teachings02.html.

Dermody, Melinda, and Susan Schleper. "Supervising: What They Didn't Teach You in Library School." *College and Research Libraries News* 65 (June 2004): 306–308, 332.

DesJardins, Stephen L., Dennis Ahlburg, and Brian P. McCall. "An Event History Model of Student Departure." *Economics of Education Review* 18 (1999): 375–390.

DesJardins, Stephen L., Dennis Ahlburg, and Brian P. McCall. "A Temporal Investigation of Factors Related to Timely Degree Completion." *Journal of Higher Education* 73 (September/October 2002): 555–581.

Epstein, Carmen. "Using Blackboard for Training and Communicating with Student Employees." *College and Undergraduate Libraries* 10, 1 (2003): 21–25.

Fuller, F. Jay. "Employing Library Student Assistants as Student Supervisors." *College and Research Libraries News* 9 (October 1990): 855–857.

Giesecke, Joan. "Performance Appraisal." In *Practical Help for New Supervisors*. Edited by Joan Giesecke. Chicago: American Library Association, 1992.

Gregory, David. "The Evolving Role of Student Employees in Academic Libraries." *Journal of Library Administration* 21, 3/4 (1995): 3–27.

Halsted, Deborah, and Dana Neely. "The Importance of the Library Technician." *Library Journal* (March 1, 1990): 62–63.

Hayes, Jan, and Maureen Sullivan. "Mapping the Process: Engaging Staff in Work Redesign." *Library Administration and Management* 17, 2 (Spring 2003): 87–93.

Henning, M. M. "Expanding the Role of the Student Desk Assistant in the Electronic Environment." *College and Undergraduate Libraries* 7, Number 1 (2000): 11–24.

Herzberg, Frederick. "One More Time: How Do You Motivate Employees?" *Harvard Business Review* 46 (January/February 1968): 53–62.

Howe, Neil, and William Strauss. *Millennials Rising: The Next Great Generation*. New York: Vintage Books, 2000.

Jennerich, Elaine, and Edward Jennerich. *Reference Interview as Creative Art*, 2nd edition. Englewood, CO: Libraries Unlimited, 1997.

Jerabek, Ann. "Job Descriptions: Don't Hire Without Them." *Journal of Interlibrary Loan, Document Delivery and Information Supply* 13, 3 (2003): 113–126.

Kalinsky, Geri, and Elizabeth Plummer. "Interviewing and Hiring Workshop." Human Resources Division, New York University. Photocopy.

Kaye, Beverly L., and Sharon Jordan-Evans. "New Hires: Getting the Right Fit." *Credit Union Executive Journal* 41, 2 (March/April 2001): 32–24.

Kerkvliet, Joe, and Clifford Nowell. "Does One Size Fit All? University Differences in the Influence of Wages, Financial Aid and Integration on Student Retention." *Economics of Education Review* 24 (2005): 89–95.

Lancaster, Lynne, and David Stillman. "From World War II to the World Wide Web: Traditionalists, Baby Boomers Generation Xers and Millennials at Work." *Women in Business* 55 (November/December 2003): 33–36.

Legault, Marie. "Caution: Mixed Generations at Work." *Canadian HR Reporter* 16, 21 (December 1, 2003): 23–24.

Letarte, Karen M., Charles Pennell, and Shirley Hamlett. "Creating Career Paths for Cataloging Support Staff." In *Innovative Redesign and Reorganization of Library Technical Services: Paths for the Future and Case Studies*. Edited by Bradford Lee Eden. Westport, CT: Libraries Unlimited, 2004.

Lin, Yei Fang, and Brian H. Kleiner. "How to Hire Employees Effectively." *Management Research News* 27, 4/5 (2004): 108–115.

Lukas, Robert R. "A Skeptic Tries It and Likes It." *Inform* 5 (1992): 27.

Marshall, Jeffrey. "Managing Different Generations at Work." *Financial Executive* 20, 5 (July/August 2004): 18.

Martin, Cheryl. "Workflow Analysis as a Basis for Organizational Redesign at McMaster University Library." In *Innovative Redesign and Reorganization of Library Technical Services: Paths for the Future and Case Studies*. Edited byBradford Lee Eden. Westport, CT: Libraries Unlimited, 2004.

Maslow, Abraham. "A Theory of Human Motivation." *Psychological Review* 50 (July 1943): 370–396.

Maxwell, Jan. "Managing Change." In *Practical Help for New Supervisors*. Edited by Joan Giesecke. Chicago. American Library Association, 1992.

Moeller-Peifer, Kathleen. "Communication." In *Practical Help for New Supervisors*. Edited by Joan Gieseke. Chicago: American Library Association, 1992.

Nagel, Mary, and Jeanne Malloy. "In Praise of Students as Supervisors." *College and Research Libraries News* 9 (October 1991): 577–578.

Nelson, Bob, and Peter Economy. *Managing for Dummies*. Foster City, CA: IDG Books, 1996.

Padilla, Irene M., and Thomas Patterson. "Rewarding Employees Nonmonetarily." In *Practical Help for New Supervisors*. Edited by Joan Giesecke. Chicago: American Library Association, 1992.

Patterson, Maureen. "Overcoming the Hiring Crunch: Tests Deliver Informed Choices." *Employment Relations Today* 27, 3 (Autumn 2000): 77.

Rimmer, Anne. "Interviewing." In *Practical Help for New Supervisors*. Edited by Joan Giesecke. Chicago: American Library Association, 1992.

Rubin, Richard. *Foundations of Library and Information Science*. New York: Neal-Schuman, 1997.

Russell, Thyra K. "Student Employment Manuals." *Journal of Library Administration* 21, 3/4 (1995): 95–108.

Slagell, Jeff, and Jeanne Langendorfer. "Don't Tread on Me: The Art of Supervising Student Assistants." *The Serials Librarian* 44 (2003): 279–284.

Stueart, Robert D., and Barbara B. Moran. *Library and Information Center Management*, 5th edition. Englewood, CO: Libraries Unlimited, 1998.

Sullivan, Maureen. "Reflections on Academic Libraries as Self-Organizing Systems: Ways Leaders Can Support Staff." *ACRL News* 60, 5 (May 1999): 393–394.

Systems, Procedures and Exchange Center, Association of Research Libraries. *Student Employment in ARL Libraries* (Kit 168). Washington, DC: ARL, 1990.

"Techniques Interviews Author Neil Howe About Millennials in the Workplace." *Techniques* 76, 6 (Spring 2003): 51.

Turner, Anne M. "Making Personnel Studies Work." *Library Journal* (2003): 54.

United States Department of Education. Office of Educational Research and Improvement. National Center for Education Statistics. *The Status of Academic Libraries in the United States: Results from the 1996 Academic Library Survey with Historical Comparisons.* Prepared by Maggie Cahalan, Wendy Mansfield and Natalie Justh. NCES 2001-301. Washington, DC: U.S. Department of Education, May 2001.

Wilson, Christine, and John Folz. "Managing Multiple Generations at Work." *Feed and Grain* 44 (August/September 2005): 54–60.

Zeller, Shawn. "The Perfect Candidate." *Government Executive* 37, 11 (July 1, 2005): 40–46.

SOURCE B: WEB LINKS TO RECOMMENDED POLICIES AND PROCEDURES

GENERAL STUDENT WORKER PROGRAM DESCRIPTIONS AND POLICIES

The Seattle Public Library

March 11, 2006

Home   Start Pages   Using the Library   Library Collection   Events & Classes   Locations   **About the Library**

About the Library
Library Careers : Library Jobs

About the Library	< Back to Library Jobs
Contact Us	❖ Employment Application Instructions
Feedback Form	❖ Employee Benefits
Mission Statement	❖ More About Employment at The Seattle Public Library
Library Careers	❖ Tips for Applicants

JOB APPLICATION FORM
Secure interactive job application.

Employee Benefits

More About Employment at The Seattle Public Library

Tips for Applicants

Title: Student Assistant

Application Deadline : Not currently open for application

Job Number : STA

Pay Range : $10.26 - $13.68 per hour

Hours : Varies between 12 and 15 hours per week and includes working weekday afternoons and evenings, and rotating Saturdays and/or Sundays.

Overview : Applications will only be accepted each year at these times:
August 1 - September 30
April 1 - May 31

Why Work at the Library

Library Jobs

Library School Scholarship

Libraries for All Building Program

Library History & Facts

Figure B-1. Seattle Public Library Student Assistant Program

You must use the <u>Student Assistant Program Employment Application</u> (not the general Library job application) to apply for the Student Assistant position. See instructions below on how to apply.

The Student Assistant Program

Are you currently enrolled in school? Are you looking for an enriching employment experience? Do you like working with people from all different backgrounds, learning new things, and participating on a team? Then keep reading!

The Seattle Public Library invites applications from high school, vocational/technical school and college students for its Student Assistant Program which is primarily designed for students who might have difficulties reaching their educational goals without the assistance of steady employment. The program prepares students for entry into the world of employment by providing them with real-life work experience and teaching them marketable skills. We are looking for applicants who would welcome experience working with diverse clientele and staff, providing customer service, and meeting and mastering new challenges. The Library seeks students who can commit to participating in this work experience and training/internship, as follows:

1. Work Locations - Student Assistants work in the Central Library, the Washington Talking Book & Braille Library, or one of 23 Library branches. An effort will be made to place students according to the their preferences; however, students must be aware that this accommodation may not be possible in every case. Students who are most willing and able to be flexible and work at ANY Library location will receive first consideration in the hiring process. Student Assistants may be rotated between locations to gain experience working in different services and programs, and are expected to be flexible toward such reassignments.

2. Job Duties - Job duties include: sorting, shelving, and retrieving books and other materials; checking materials in and out; processing materials for use; sorting and routing materials by Dewey decimal and alpha and numerical schemes; and occasionally helping to provide service to Library patrons at public desks or support duties. Some assignments may involve working in one of the Library's many computer labs, assisting Library visitors (patrons) in using PC's and the Internet.

3. Training and Development - students selected will receive paid training in basic job duties, required work skills, and library services and programs. Other developmental experiences provided during the student's three-year program include special developmental training and workshops on topics such as customer service and diversity, goal setting, team building, self-esteem, effective communication, and possible internship placements. Student Assistants are Temporary Employees and may participate in the program for no more than three years OR until they no longer qualify as students. Student Assistants start at the first step of the salary range and receive salary increases as they successfully participate in the program, until the top step is reached. The program operates throughout the year, and students may have an opportunity to work additional hours during official school breaks for holidays, Spring Break, and during the summer.

Library News Releases

Leaders & Organizations

Library Use Policies

Support Your Library

Figure B-1. Seattle Public Library Student Assistant Program *(Continued)*

How are students chosen?

All applications received will be carefully reviewed, and the strongest candidates will be invited to participate in a written test. Those successful in that test will be invited to an oral interview. The candidates who are selected through this process will receive PAID basic training and orientation. Once trained, the Student Assistant is NOT guaranteed immediate placement in a job, but may be placed on a roster (or list) from which future vacancies may be filled. Vacancies arise at various times; it isn't possible to predict when. Placement in a job may happen at any time during the year.

Essential Functions :

- Job duties include: sorting, shelving, and retrieving books and other materials; checking materials in and out; processing materials for use; sorting and routing materials by Dewey decimal and alpha and numerical schemes; and occasionally helping to provide service to Library patrons at public desks or support duties. Some assignments may involve working in one of the Library's many computer labs, assisting Library visitors (patrons) in using PC's and the Internet.

Required Qualifications :

- **To be eligible for this program, applicants must:**

  - Be 16 years of age or older and be enrolled in high school, college, an accredited vocational/technical school or equivalent training program, or a G.E.D. program. (Students who have already attained a Bachelor's degree from college are NOT ELIGIBLE for this program.)
  - Be able to work between 12 and 15 hours per week, including some weekday afternoons and evenings until 8:00 p.m., and, on a rotating basis, between 10 a.m. and 6 p.m. on Saturdays, and on Sunday afternoons between 1 p.m. and 5 p.m.
  - Be able to produce: proof of school enrollment; personal identification (such as a driver's license or Washington State Department of Licensing I.D., birth certificate, or similar identification); and a valid Social Security Card.

- **Candidates will be screened for the following abilities to:**

  - Communicate effectively with staff and patrons, and to follow written and verbal instructions accurately.
  - Sort materials alphabetically and numerically, including numbers with decimals. (Student Assistants will learn Dewey decimal and other sorting methods through on-the-job training. However, candidates must have the ability to sort by alphabet and by numbers in decimal form and to follow basic written instructions. Candidates will be tested for these skills.)
  - Learn and apply basic procedures for the Library's automated circulation and catalog systems.
  - Adapt to rapidly changing priorities, procedures and situations.
  - Work as a team member with a diverse group of employees and patrons.
  - Work afternoon, evening and weekend schedules and the willingness to work in a variety of library locations.
  - PC skills are not required, but are desirable, especially the ability to use the Internet and the WWW to access information.

Figure B-1. Seattle Public Library Student Assistant Program *(Continued)*

How to apply : Print out a copy of this job bulletin and the following Student Assistant Employment Application materials and read the qualifications carefully.

Please submit all your materials together, at the same time. An incomplete application could disqualify you from consideration, so BE SURE TO FOLLOW THESE INSTRUCTIONS CAREFULLY.

All of the following must be submitted:

1. Student Assistant Program Employment Application
The Seattle Public Library Student Assistant Program Employment Application must be submitted for consideration for current and future openings. In that application, you should fully describe any volunteer or school activity or experiences that relate to providing service or working in teams.
You must use the Student Assistant Program Employment Application (not the general Library job application) to apply for the Student Assistant position.

2. Proof of School Enrollment
This can include a copy of a current student body ID card, a letter from a school vocational counselor, or a school official's statement of enrollment. This information may be verified prior to employment and at other times during employment because only those who are currently enrolled in and attending school may be employed in this program. Students employed in this program will have to provide this information to the Human Resources Department each quarter that they are in the program, to verify their continuing eligibility as students.

3. Cover Letter
Attach all of the required application materials to a cover letter which:
- Tells us something about yourself. We are particularly interested in knowing why you are interested in working in the Library's Student Assistant Program and how it would help you pursue your education and vocational goals.
- Tells us about any barriers you face to obtaining or continuing your education.
- Includes the date when you anticipate you will be graduating and how long you plan to participate in the program if you are selected.

4. Referral Form
This form is included in this packet and must be completed by an instructor or supervisor with appropriate contact information and signature and sealed in an envelope. Once completed please attach with other application materials.

THE SEATTLE PUBLIC LIBRARY PROUDLY PROMOTES DIVERSITY IN EMPLOYMENT.
If accommodations are needed during the selection process, please let us know.

Privacy   Web Site Help   Site Index   Library Careers   Contact Us
© 2006 The Seattle Public Library 1000 Fourth Ave., Seattle, WA 98104-1109

http://www.spl.org/default.asp?pageID=about_jobsvolunteering_jobs_openings_detail&cid=1090622867886

Figure B-1. Seattle Public Library Student Assistant Program *(Continued)*

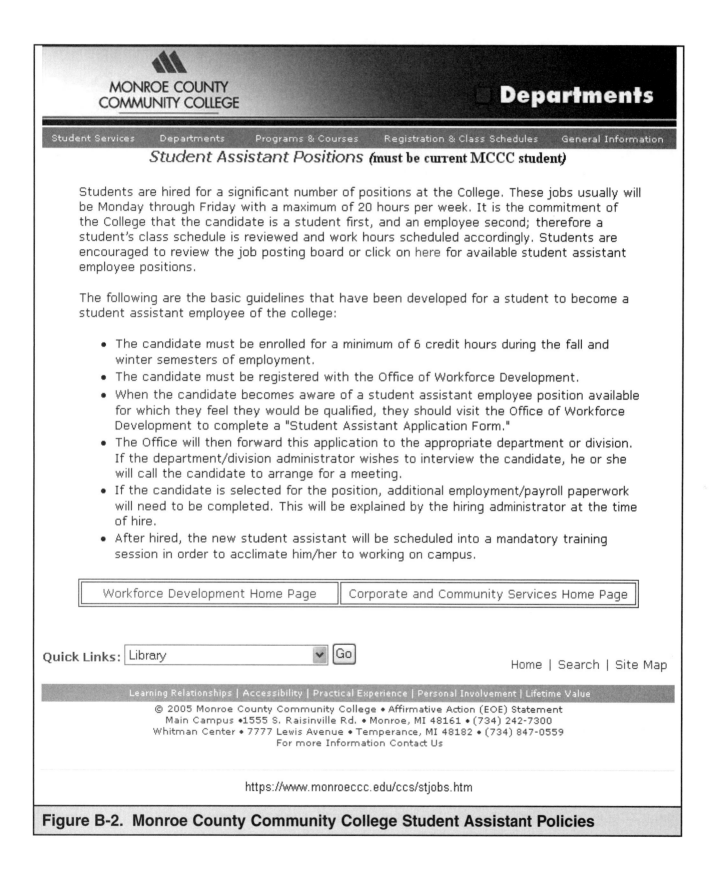

Figure B-2. Monroe County Community College Student Assistant Policies

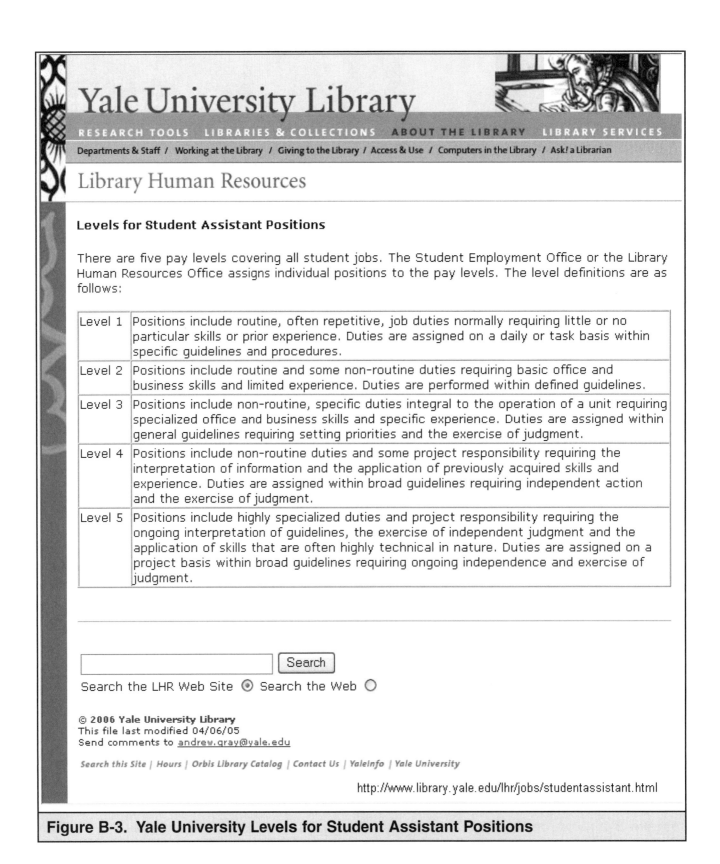

Yale University Library

RESEARCH TOOLS   LIBRARIES & COLLECTIONS   ABOUT THE LIBRARY   LIBRARY SERVICES
Departments & Staff / Working at the Library / Giving to the Library / Access & Use / Computers in the Library / Ask! a Librarian

Library Human Resources

Levels for Student Assistant Positions

There are five pay levels covering all student jobs. The Student Employment Office or the Library Human Resources Office assigns individual positions to the pay levels. The level definitions are as follows:

Level 1	Positions include routine, often repetitive, job duties normally requiring little or no particular skills or prior experience. Duties are assigned on a daily or task basis within specific guidelines and procedures.
Level 2	Positions include routine and some non-routine duties requiring basic office and business skills and limited experience. Duties are performed within defined guidelines.
Level 3	Positions include non-routine, specific duties integral to the operation of a unit requiring specialized office and business skills and specific experience. Duties are assigned within general guidelines requiring setting priorities and the exercise of judgment.
Level 4	Positions include non-routine duties and some project responsibility requiring the interpretation of information and the application of previously acquired skills and experience. Duties are assigned within broad guidelines requiring independent action and the exercise of judgment.
Level 5	Positions include highly specialized duties and project responsibility requiring the ongoing interpretation of guidelines, the exercise of independent judgment and the application of skills that are often highly technical in nature. Duties are assigned on a project basis within broad guidelines requiring ongoing independence and exercise of judgment.

[Search field] [Search]

Search the LHR Web Site ⊙ Search the Web ○

© 2006 Yale University Library
This file last modified 04/06/05
Send comments to andrew.gray@yale.edu

Search this Site | Hours | Orbis Library Catalog | Contact Us | YaleInfo | Yale University

http://www.library.yale.edu/lhr/jobs/studentassistant.html

Figure B-3. Yale University Levels for Student Assistant Positions

STUDENT WORKER PLANNING TOOLS

Penn Library
Public Service Student Assistant
Position Description

Position Title: _____

Date: _____

Library: _____

Unit: _____

Primary Supervisor(s): _____

Total number of student hours needed: _____

Check all that apply:
☐ Early morning   ☐ Morning   ☐ Afternoon
☐ Evening   ☐ Late Night   ☐ Weekend

Position Summary:

_____

_____

_____

Duties:

☐ Assist patrons w/services/procedures   ☐ Research assistance
☐ Circulation   ☐ Equipment troubleshooting
☐ Shelve materials   ☐ Search materials
☐ Retrieve materials   ☐ Clerical
☐ Shelf read/shift materials   ☐ Photocopying/Scanning
☐ Other   ☐ _____
☐ _____   ☐ _____
☐ _____   ☐ _____

Check all that apply:
Supervised?:   ☐ Yes   ☐ No   ☐ Some Hours
Schedule: ☐ Fixed   ☐ Flexible

http://staffweb.library.upenn.edu//hr/studentasst/template-job.doc

Figure B-4. University of Pennsylvania Public Services Student Assistant Position Description

SAMPLE SCHEDULING TOOLS

📖Van Pelt Library📖
Access Services
Schedule Agreement

This schedule is for the entire semester. If you do not show up to work during the final exam period, you may not be eligible for rehire the following semester. If you are unable to work an assigned shift, please follow the Substitution procedure. If you need to make a change in your schedule, please speak to your supervisor.

Schedule:

Mondays: _____

Tuesdays: _____

Wednesdays: _____

Thursdays: _____

Fridays: _____

Saturdays: _____

Sundays: _____

I understand and accept the following responsibilities:

Signed: _____ **Date:** _____

http://staffweb.library.upenn.edu//hr/studentasst/schedule-agreement.doc

Figure B-5. University of Pennsylvania Schedule Agreement

| University *of* Florida | Hours | Ask a Librarian | Online Requests | Remote Logon |
| George A. Smathers Libraries | Library Catalog | Databases | Site Map | Help | Search |

Library › Staff Web › Humanities and Social Sciences Services Department › H&SS Smathers Library Student Assistant Schedule

H&SS Smathers Library Student Assistant Schedule Spring 2006

Circulation/Shelving

	Sunday	Monday	Tuesday	Wednesday	Thursday	Friday
8:00-9:00		Maureen	Allen	Maureen	Allen	Allen
9:00-10:00		Maureen	Allen	Maureen	Allen	Allen
10:00-11:00		Maureen	Allen	Maureen	Allen	Allen
11:00-12:00		Stefanie	Allen	Maureen	Candace	Stefanie
12:00-1:00		Sisteria	Candace	Candace	Candace	Sisteria
1:00-2:00	Sarah	Sisteria	Candace	Candace	Candace	Sisteria
2:00-3:00	Sarah	Sisteria	Sola	Sola	Sola	Sisteria
3:00-4:00	Sarah	Sisteria	Sola	Sola	Sola	Sisteria
4:00-5:00	Sarah	Sisteria	Sola	Sola	Sola	Sisteria
5:00-6:00	Sarah	Sisteria	Sola	Sola	Sola	Sisteria
6:00-9:00	Samsad	Brian	Brian	Brian	Brian	

Phones

	Sunday	Monday	Tuesday	Wednesday	Thursday	Friday
9:00-12:00		Jamie (9:30)	Hillary	Jamie (9:30)	Hillary	Maureen
2:00-5:00		Andrea	Hillary	Andrea	Andrea	Andrea

Off-Desk

	Sunday	Monday	Tuesday	Wednesday	Thursday	Friday
Danielle			10:30-4:00		11:30-4:00	
Stefanie		12:00-3:00		3:00-5:00		12:00-3:00
Matt			8:00-3:30		8:00-3:30	

Instruction (Off-Season Hours)

	Sunday	Monday	Tuesday	Wednesday	Thursday	Friday
Kris			TBA		TBA	
Yancy		3:00-6:00			12:00-3:00	9:30-12:30
Kathleen		12:30-3:30	10:00-1:00			
Samsad			11:00-3:00	2:00-5:00		
Jamie		9:30-1:30		9:30-1:30		9:30-1:30

Staff Web | Staff Directory | Departments | Privacy Policy

UNIVERSITY OF FLORIDA

http://www.uflib.ufl.edu/hss/staff/studentsched.html

Figure B-6. University of Florida Student Assistant Schedule

SAMPLE STUDENT WORKER ORIENTATION MATERIALS AND HANDBOOKS

 UNIVERSITY LIBRARIES

How do I...?   Site Index A-Z   Search

| Home | Catalog | Research Port | ? Ask us! |

LEARNING ORGANIZATION

▶ Personnel Programs

▶ Organizational Development

▶ Learning Curriculum

  ▶Staff Learning and Development

ADMINISTRATIVE

▶Frequently-Asked-Questions (FAQ)

▶ Administrative Memo Series

▶**UM Libraries' New Student Assistants Orientation Survey**

▶ Library Personnel and Budget

▶ Information for People with Disabilities

▶ Helping Students in Distress (PDF)

▶UM Human Resources

▶ **Student Assistant Handbook**

Personnel Programs > University of Maryland Libraries' Student Assistant Orientation

University of Maryland Libraries' Student Assistant Orientation

Welcome to New University of Maryland Libraries' Student Assistants

University Maryland Libraries' Orientation Program:

The New Staff Orientation Program is designed to welcome and equip each new library staff member with information that will enhance their ability to perform assigned duties and responsibilities, and to ensure their success in the Library workplace. In keeping with the University's Orientation policy, the Libraries' New Staff Orientation is a required informal information-sharing program that serves as a critical tool for acclimating staff to the library as well as to the University community. It also provides each new employee the opportunity to get an overview of the Libraries' concept of the learning organization, and its commitment to the principle of continuous improvement and life long learning. Therefore, it is the responsibility of each new library staff member to take advantage of this valuable tool and process.

The overall program includes the following areas of special interest to new staff:

- Orientation to Payroll and Benefits
  (Enrollment for employment with Lupe Fernandes)
- Orientation to assigned Division, Department, Unit, and Job
  (To be completed by your immediate supervisor)

Figure B-7. University of Maryland Student Assistant Orientation

▶ Voluntary Resignation Policy

▶ Acronym List for Library Teams

▶ 2005-2006 University Holiday Schedule

ORIENTATIONS FOR:

▶ University of Maryland Libraries Student Assistant Orientation

- Overview of the Libraries' mission, services, policies and procedures, programs, performance review, professional development opportunities and plans
  (To be completed with me, Johnnie Love, Coordinator of Personnel Programs)

The New Staff Orientation program is designed to address concerns of each group of employees: new library faculty, staff, graduate assistant, and student assistant. Each new staff member receives an orientation letter from Johnnie Love, the Coordinator of Personnel Programs. The Coordinator for Recruitment, Lupe Fernandes, also shares information about new staff orientation as each new staff member completes their personnel paperwork and benefits information.

STUDENT ASSISTANTS HANDBOOK

Click on: **Student Assistant Handbook.** and Frequently Asked Questions. Student Assistants: ASK and core competencies for Student Assistants.

return to top

▲

University Libraries, University of Maryland, College Park, MD 20742-7011 (301)405-0800
Please send comments and suggestions to the Libraries' Webmaster.
Content questions should be directed to Information Provider
Last modified: December 15, 2005

© 2005 University of Maryland Libraries
Last Revised: August 2005

http://www.lib.umd.edu/groups/learning/librarystudentassistantorientation.html

Figure B-7. University of Maryland Student Assistant Orientation *(Continued)*

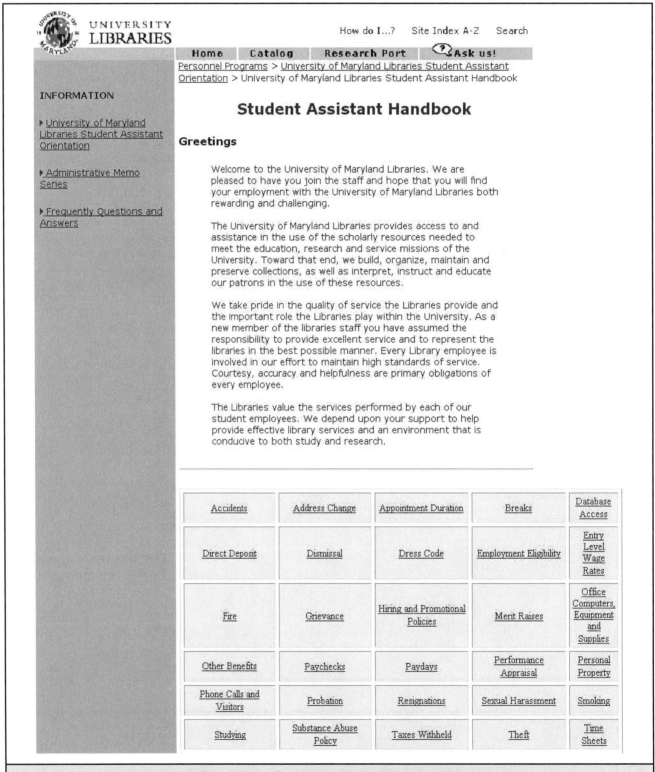

Figure B-8. University of Maryland Student Assistant Handbook

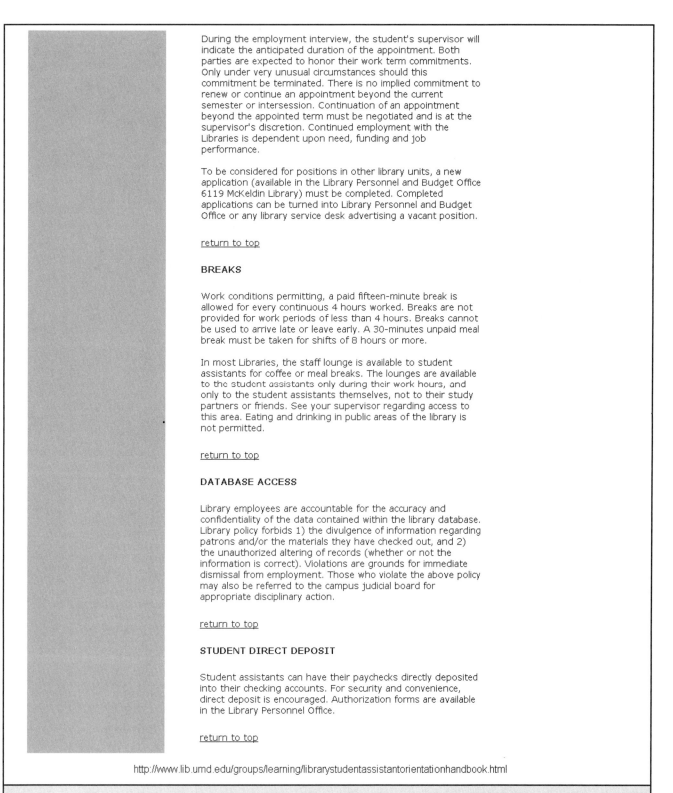

During the employment interview, the student's supervisor will indicate the anticipated duration of the appointment. Both parties are expected to honor their work term commitments. Only under very unusual circumstances should this commitment be terminated. There is no implied commitment to renew or continue an appointment beyond the current semester or intersession. Continuation of an appointment beyond the appointed term must be negotiated and is at the supervisor's discretion. Continued employment with the Libraries is dependent upon need, funding and job performance.

To be considered for positions in other library units, a new application (available in the Library Personnel and Budget Office 6119 McKeldin Library) must be completed. Completed applications can be turned into Library Personnel and Budget Office or any library service desk advertising a vacant position.

return to top

BREAKS

Work conditions permitting, a paid fifteen-minute break is allowed for every continuous 4 hours worked. Breaks are not provided for work periods of less than 4 hours. Breaks cannot be used to arrive late or leave early. A 30-minutes unpaid meal break must be taken for shifts of 8 hours or more.

In most Libraries, the staff lounge is available to student assistants for coffee or meal breaks. The lounges are available to the student assistants only during their work hours, and only to the student assistants themselves, not to their study partners or friends. See your supervisor regarding access to this area. Eating and drinking in public areas of the library is not permitted.

return to top

DATABASE ACCESS

Library employees are accountable for the accuracy and confidentiality of the data contained within the library database. Library policy forbids 1) the divulgence of information regarding patrons and/or the materials they have checked out, and 2) the unauthorized altering of records (whether or not the information is correct). Violations are grounds for immediate dismissal from employment. Those who violate the above policy may also be referred to the campus judicial board for appropriate disciplinary action.

return to top

STUDENT DIRECT DEPOSIT

Student assistants can have their paychecks directly deposited into their checking accounts. For security and convenience, direct deposit is encouraged. Authorization forms are available in the Library Personnel Office.

return to top

http://www.lib.umd.edu/groups/learning/librarystudentassistantorientationhandbook.html

Figure B-8. University of Maryland Student Assistant Handbook *(Continued)*

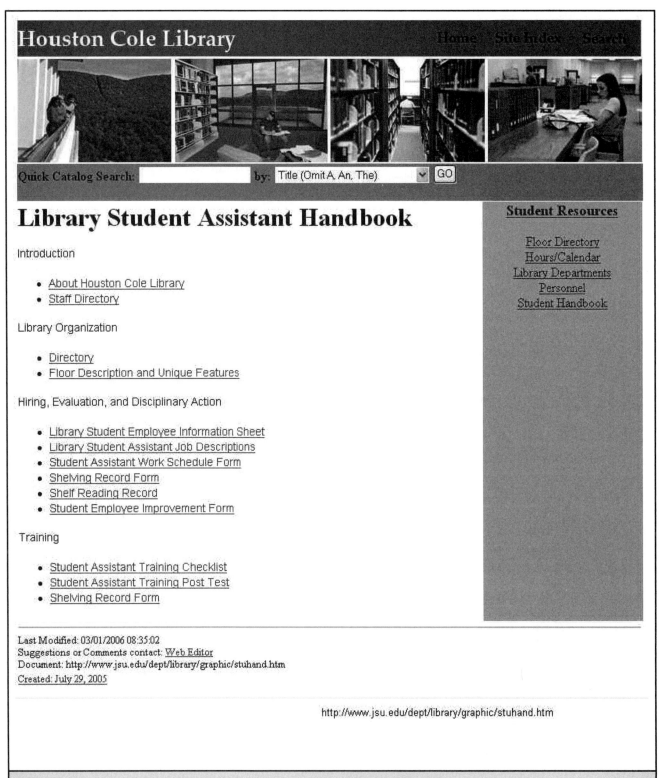

Figure B-9. Jackson State University Assistant Handbook

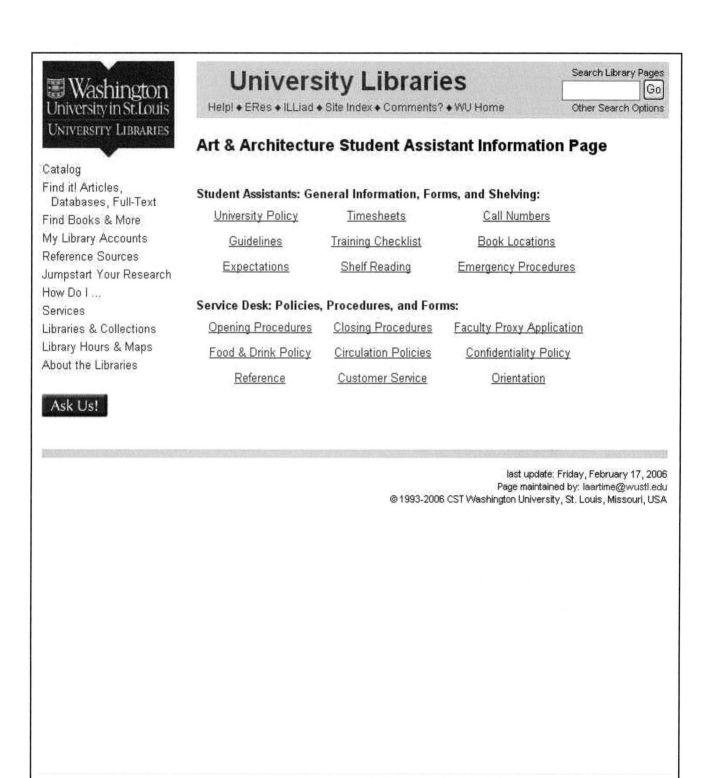

Figure B-10. Washington University Student Assistant Information Page

SAMPLE TRAINING MATERIALS

University of Pennsylvania
Student Assistant Customer Service Expectations

Be Dependable & Punctual.
Example:
Call your supervisor if you cannot make it to work. Don't rely on sending e-mail.

Be Available/Let users know you are here to serve them.
Examples:
Be friendly.
If you are attending a service desk, refrain from doing personal work or games at the computer unless you have discussed it with your supervisor; refrain from using headphones. If you are doing work while attending the desk, be sure to look up throughout your shift to see if anyone appears to need help.
If someone looks like they might need help, consider offering assistance even if they haven't asked.

Respond Promptly.
Examples:
Answer the phone within a reasonable number of rings.
If there is a line at the service desk, reassure those in line that you will be with them shortly.
If you can't answer a question, seek help right away or refer the patron elsewhere.
Let users know what you're doing for them if it's taking a while.

Be Accurate and Thorough.
Examples:
Know where to find Library policies and procedures on the web or in a manual.
Check with users to make sure you've answered their question.
Don't hesitate to seek help from a librarian or full-time staff member.
If staff is not available and you can't answer a question, offer to have someone contact the person later or make a referral to another library if it seems appropriate.
Remember, Penn has 15 libraries!

Be Professional: Remember that you represent the Penn Library system.
Examples:
If you're aware of a problem in the library, inform full time staff.
Don't talk about patrons.
If a patron is angry or being difficult, remain composed and polite and seek assistance from full-time staff.

http://staffweb.library.upenn.edu//hr/studentasst/stud-worker-cust-stds.doc

---

Figure B-11. University of Pennsylvania Student Assistant Customer Service Expectation

📖Penn Library📖
Student Employment Agreement

The Library agrees to employ you through the coming term, provided that the requirements set here are met. By accepting employment at the Penn Library, you agree to:

- be responsible for the policies and procedures covered in your training, including procedures related to the Library's Confidentiality policy.
- put your role as library employee first, and not socialize while on duty.
- be consistent, even, and polite in your service to all library users.
- refrain from using cell phones and receiving non-emergency phone calls.
- keep food and drink in approved areas only.
- maintain your schedule for the entire semester as agreed upon with your supervisor.
- follow established substitution procedures in order to temporarily change your schedule.
- refrain from loading any software on library computers, and or altering workstations in any way.
- report hours worked accurately in order to avoid dismissal on the grounds of theft of hours.
- read the Student Manual you were issued.

Failure to meet these guidelines could result in progressive discipline and/or termination of employment.

I understand and accept the responsibilities listed above.

Signed: _____   **Date:** _____

http://staffweb.library.upenn.edu//hr/studentasst/employment-agreement.doc

Figure B-12. University of Pennsylvania Student Employment Agreement

University of Louisville Libraries

Student Assistant Training Program

Student Training Checklist

The following is a checklist that supervisors should print off and use to keep track of the training the new student assistant has received.

Student:	Start date:

☐ **Paperwork cleared through Administrative Office**
- Payroll/Personnel Data Sheet complete
- Verification of employment eligibility

☐ **Time cards/time sheets**
- how to clock in, how to correct clock in errors
- where and when to pick up paychecks

☐ **Introductions** to ...
- other students and staff in the dept.
- important places: restroom, staff lounge, emergency exit

☐ **Tour of the Library** and concept of the 7 libraries

Materials and exercises for this section are available from the **Student Assistant Training Program** web page at http://www.louisville.edu/library/training/.

☐ **Student Assistant Handbook**
- give student a personal copy of the handbook
- Handbook exercise - completed (date):_____

☐ **Patron Service Seminar**
- attended (date): _____
- if unable to attend, read through materials on (date): _____

☐ **Public Service Dictionary**
- instructed on what the PSD is and its nearest locations (print and web)
- PSD exercise - completed (date): _____

☐ **Minerva 2000**
- Minerva training checklist, completed (date): _____
- or, attended Minerva jumpstart session: _____

☐ **Shelving Introduction**
- read through Proper Care and Handling of Books
- read through Reading Library of Congress Call Numbers
- Shelving Books - Review Exercise, completed: _____

☐ **Informed of Performance Appraisal procedures**

http://www.louisville.edu/library/training/check.htm

Figure B-13. University of Louisville Student Training Checklist

Houston Cole Library

Student Employee Improvement Form

Date: _____

Name: _____

To ensure that you receive a good evaluation at the end of the semester, it is suggested that you improve your job performance in the following area(s):

_____ Late to work
_____ Absence from work
_____ Remaining at your workstation
_____ Picking up books in lobby upon arrival to work
_____ Shelving
_____ Filing
_____ Reading shelves
_____ Patron complaints
_____ Other as listed

Other comments: _____
_____
_____
_____

Suggestions for improvement: _____
_____
_____
_____

Please contact the following if you need further information or assistance:
Name _____
Telephone _____
e-mail _____
Available hours _____

To Library Student Assistant Handbook

To Library Home Page

To JSU Homepage

Last Update: December 2, 2003
Suggestions or Comments contact: Doug Taylor or Jodi Poe

http://www.jsu.edu/dept/library/graphic/simprove.htm

Figure B-14. Jackson State University Student Employment Improvement Form

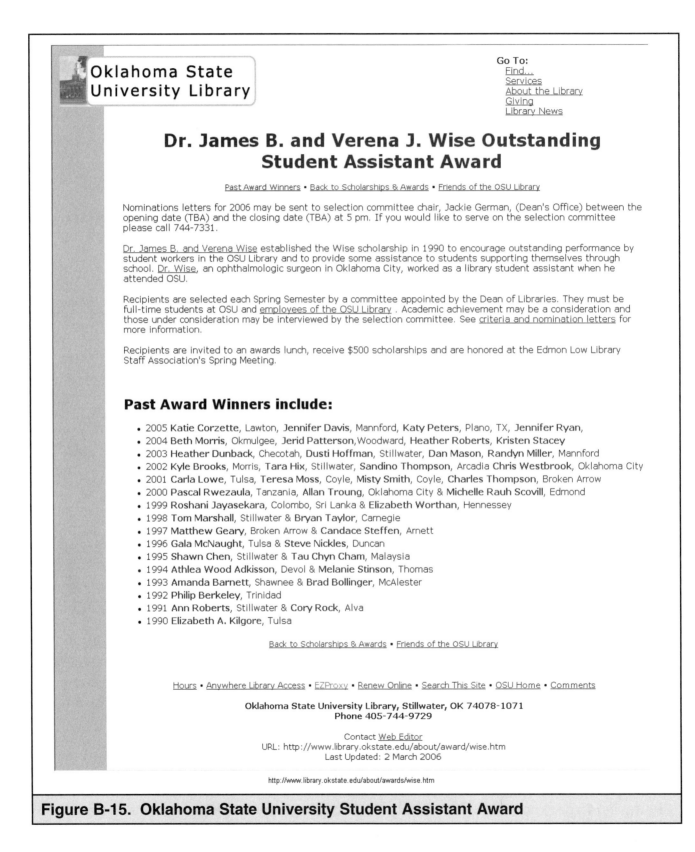

Go To:
Find...
Services
About the Library
Giving
Library News

Oklahoma State University Library

Dr. James B. and Verena J. Wise Outstanding Student Assistant Award

Past Award Winners • Back to Scholarships & Awards • Friends of the OSU Library

Nominations letters for 2006 may be sent to selection committee chair, Jackie German, (Dean's Office) between the opening date (TBA) and the closing date (TBA) at 5 pm. If you would like to serve on the selection committee please call 744-7331.

Dr. James B. and Verena Wise established the Wise scholarship in 1990 to encourage outstanding performance by student workers in the OSU Library and to provide some assistance to students supporting themselves through school. Dr. Wise, an ophthalmologic surgeon in Oklahoma City, worked as a library student assistant when he attended OSU.

Recipients are selected each Spring Semester by a committee appointed by the Dean of Libraries. They must be full-time students at OSU and employees of the OSU Library . Academic achievement may be a consideration and those under consideration may be interviewed by the selection committee. See criteria and nomination letters for more information.

Recipients are invited to an awards lunch, receive $500 scholarships and are honored at the Edmon Low Library Staff Association's Spring Meeting.

Past Award Winners include:

- 2005 **Katie Corzette**, Lawton, **Jennifer Davis**, Mannford, **Katy Peters**, Plano, TX, **Jennifer Ryan**,
- 2004 **Beth Morris**, Okmulgee, **Jerid Patterson**,Woodward, **Heather Roberts**, **Kristen Stacey**
- 2003 **Heather Dunback**, Checotah, **Dusti Hoffman**, Stillwater, **Dan Mason**, **Randyn Miller**, Mannford
- 2002 **Kyle Brooks**, Morris, **Tara Hix**, Stillwater, **Sandino Thompson**, Arcadia **Chris Westbrook**, Oklahoma City
- 2001 **Carla Lowe**, Tulsa, **Teresa Moss**, Coyle, **Misty Smith**, Coyle, **Charles Thompson**, Broken Arrow
- 2000 **Pascal Rwezaula**, Tanzania, **Allan Troung**, Oklahoma City & **Michelle Rauh Scovill**, Edmond
- 1999 **Roshani Jayasekara**, Colombo, Sri Lanka & **Elizabeth Worthan**, Hennessey
- 1998 **Tom Marshall**, Stillwater & **Bryan Taylor**, Carnegie
- 1997 **Matthew Geary**, Broken Arrow & **Candace Steffen**, Arnett
- 1996 **Gala McNaught**, Tulsa & **Steve Nickles**, Duncan
- 1995 **Shawn Chen**, Stillwater & **Tau Chyn Cham**, Malaysia
- 1994 **Athlea Wood Adkisson**, Devol & **Melanie Stinson**, Thomas
- 1993 **Amanda Barnett**, Shawnee & **Brad Bollinger**, McAlester
- 1992 **Philip Berkeley**, Trinidad
- 1991 **Ann Roberts**, Stillwater & **Cory Rock**, Alva
- 1990 **Elizabeth A. Kilgore**, Tulsa

Back to Scholarships & Awards • Friends of the OSU Library

Hours • Anywhere Library Access • EZProxy • Renew Online • Search This Site • OSU Home • Comments

Oklahoma State University Library, Stillwater, OK 74078-1071
Phone 405-744-9729

Contact Web Editor
URL: http://www.library.okstate.edu/about/award/wise.htm
Last Updated: 2 March 2006

http://www.library.okstate.edu/about/awards/wise.htm

Figure B-15. Oklahoma State University Student Assistant Award

SAMPLE SEPARATION PAPERWORK

Please complete and return to Library HR/Van Pelt, Rm. 239/6206

End of Employment Report.

Student Name _____

Library/Department _____

Date of Employment _____ to _____

Reason for End of Employment

☐ **Terminated**
Reason _____
_____
_____
_____

☐ **Not Offered Further Employment**
Reason _____
_____
_____
_____

Recommendations

☐ Not to Rehire in the Library System

☐ Not to Rehire in Unit

☐ Not to Rehire in the Public Services

☐ Other _____
_____
_____

Submitted By _____ Date _____

http://staffweb.library.upenn.edu//hr/studentasst/end-employment-rpt.doc

Figure B-16. University of Pennsylvania End of Employment Report

UC BERKELEY LIBRARY | HOME | SEARCH

Reason for leaving Library Student Employment
(to be filled out by the student employee)

Name _____

Unit _____

Email Address _____ GLADIS/INNOPAC login _____

Last date of work _____

- Please number all that apply in order of importance. Put #1 for most important.
  _____ to devote more time to studies
  _____ parents request
  _____ friendlier work environment
  _____ less stress
  _____ other employment
  _____ higher paying job on campus
  _____ higher paying job off campus
  _____ internship
  _____ withdrawing from school
  _____ graduation from school
  _____ other _____

- This form will help us determine the reasons for the turnover of our student staff. Thank you for your feedback.

- Reminder:
1. If you have had the DCP and Medicare tax taken from your paycheck, you will need to see Adria to have this money refunded to you.
2. To have your W-2 forwarded to you after you leave, please update your mailing address with Adria.
3. You may have your last paycheck mailed to you if you leave a self addressed stamped envelope with Adria.

- Fold and return this form to Adria, Student Employment, Room 110 Doe Library as soon as possible.
BY CAMPUS MAIL: Drop in campus mail. No postage necessary
Address To: Adria Christensen
Student Employment Coordinator
110 Library
m/c 6000

HELP/FAQ CATALOGS COMMENTS HOME

http://www.lib.berkeley.edu/LHRD/leaving.html

Figure B-17. University of California Berkeley Reason for Leaving Library Student Employment Form

SOURCE C: SAMPLE STUDENT WORKER HANDBOOK

ACCESS SERVICES STUDENT WORKER MANUAL: SAMPSON-LIVERMORE LIBRARY

Prepared by June Power

Welcome. We are glad to welcome you to the Sampson-Livermore Library. You are an asset to the Library; we could not operate this facility without your help. You may be surprised to learn that your job here can be an asset to you, too. You will not only gain work experience, but learn more about how to use the library effectively for your own academic endeavors. This manual provides you with general information about your job and about library policies. The full policies of the Library are covered in the Sampson-Livermore Library Policies and Procedures Manual, which you may find at the Circulation Desk. Please let me know if you have any questions after reading this manual. We look forward to working with you here in the Library.

YOU'RE IMPORTANT!

Student workers are integral to the overall function of Sampson-Livermore Library. Serving the needs of over 200 faculty in more than 30 academic departments, the collection consists of 313,145 volumes and 1,629 periodical subscriptions. The collections include software, movies, and music as well as a reference collection and electronic access to subscription databases online. It is the responsibility of Access Services to provide access to the materials that the Library owns or has access to. It is the responsibility of the Circulation Desk staff to make sure material is properly shelved, call numbers are in order, and that new services and projects are implemented as planned.

Many of the duties in Access Services require an understanding of work flow, an adherence to standards, and an attention to detail. The details of the policies and procedures of Access Services may be found in the Circulation Policies and Procedures Manual, located at the Circulation Desk. All student assistants in the department are expected to be familiar will all circulation policies and procedures.

STUDENT WORKER JOBS IN ACCESS SERVICES

STACKS MAINTANENCE

Stacks maintenance is one of the critical responsibilities of Access Services. This job entails re-shelving books after they have been checked in, performing shelf-reading to make sure books are in their proper places on the shelves, and keeping the shelves neat and tidy.

This job is extremely important to the Library and library patrons.

If materials are out of order, then the Library becomes difficult to use. If materials are not returned to the shelves promptly and/or are not found where they are supposed to be, then users become dissatisfied. Stacks maintenance helps to keep the Library functioning at a user-friendly level.

CIRCULATION DESK

At times student assistance is needed with circulation tasks. At the Circulation Desk, students assist with checking materials in and out, getting change from Lumbee Hall, answering the phone, mailing circulation notices, assisting with reserves processing, and any other library tasks with which circulation staff need assistance. When the Circulation Desk is not busy, student assistants can work on stacks maintenance or one of the tasks on the student worker to-do list. While working at the Circulation Desk does involve less physicality than other library tasks, you will be expected to be busy at all times. Working at the Circulation Desk is a privilege and not a reason for socializing or idleness.

INTERLIBRARY LOAN

Certain students are assigned to work with Interlibrary Services. These students assist with the copying, computer processing, and mailing required to complete interlibrary loan (ILL) requests. Other student workers in Access Services may also be called upon to assist with photocopying for interlibrary loan as needed. Conversely, when there is a reduction in the ILL workflow, ILL assistants will be expected to assist as needed with circulation tasks.

BENEFITS OF WORKING IN SAMPSON-LIVERMORE LIBRARY

- Flexible hours
- Valuable work experience
- Learning to be part of an organization
- Expanded knowledge of library use
- Potential for pay raises

BASIC JOB EXPECTATIONS

- Reliable Attendance
  - Arrive on time
  - If you are ill, notify the Circulation Desk Supervisor or the Access Services Librarian
  - You are responsible for finding substitutes
  - Be flexible and willing to substitute for others

- Initiative
  - Do priority work first
  - Perform additional tasks
  - Find tasks to do without being assigned to them
  - Offer suggestions for improvement

- Positive and Respectful Attitude
  - Accept assignments willingly
  - Cooperate with others
  - Contribute to a pleasant work environment

- Adherence to Library Policies and Procedures
  - Read and follow the Sampson-Livermore Library Policy and Procedures Manual
  - Always consult with the Access Services Librarian or the Circulation Desk supervisor before making exceptions to general policies
  - Never discuss confidential library matters with non-staff. This includes information about patrons, fines, books checked out, and other personal matters.
  - Computer passwords must be kept confidential

- Good Service
  - Always provide good, positive service
  - Be available and offer assistance
  - Always be pleasant—no matter how busy or stressed you are

COMMUNICATION

Team work and effective service depend upon good communication. Library patrons are customers and deserve full attention from all library employees. Pleasant manners and demeanor are important and expected at all times. Your most important skill in patron service is communication. The following tips will help:

- Make sure you understand specific tasks. Please ask questions.
- Respond promptly to all departmental communications from the Access Services Librarian or the Circulation Desk supervisors.
- Check the bulletin board regularly to be aware of any new policies, information, or problems.
- Keep your supervisor informed of your task progress.
- Encourage patron questions. If you are asked anything but a directional question, refer patrons to the reference desk.
- Inform the Circulation Desk supervisor or Access Services Librarian of any problems that occur during your shift.
- Use sound judgment when making decisions. Consult with the Circulation Desk supervisor or Access Services Librarian if uncertain.

GREETING, ASSISTANCE, AND CLOSURE

Patrons appreciate being greeted and directed to materials and equipment. Student assistants should ask if patrons need help finding books or other materials or using the computers. You can help patrons while still monitoring the Circulation Desk.

When patrons come to the Circulation Desk to check out materials, student assistants should ask, *"Did you find everything you were looking for?"* This gives you an opportunity to check their search, verify call numbers, look for items that might be misplaced on the shelf, and identify lost materials so their status can be updated. Additionally, student assistants can recommend ILL service or refer patrons to the Reference Librarian.

Student assistants can show patrons how to find specifically requested materials. However, student assistants should avoid helping select topics for projects, find ambiguous materials, interpreting data, or offering advice or opinions. These questions should always be referred to the Reference Librarian on duty. Medicine and law are particularly sensitive topic areas. Refer patrons to a librarian for more information in any uncomfortable situation.

SCHEDULES

Schedules are determined at the beginning of each semester. At this point the Access Services Librarian can determine a work schedule based around your class schedule. You must provide a copy of your schedule and desired work hours to the Access Services Librarian by the first day of classes, or date of hire if after start of term. If you will be returning to work the following semester, you may submit your pre-registration schedule early. This allows you to get the hours most convenient to your schedule. You cannot schedule yourself to work during class time.

The Access Services Librarian will notify you of the number of hours that you can work per week during the semester according to your contract and what your work schedule will be. Schedules can be changed throughout the semester if you find that the schedule you originally made is not working and the change has been approved by the Access Services Librarian. The Access Services Librarian will attempt to make the work schedule fit your convenience as far as possible, but department needs, seniority, and other considerations are also determining factors in scheduling.

Students are not expected to work during university breaks; this time is optional. You should inform the Access Services Librarian prior to this time of whether you intend to work or not. Separate schedules can be made up for this time as well. Separate schedules are also made for finals week. A scheduling book will be placed in the student worker area with instructions.

You are expected to work your scheduled hours, as both other assistants and the circulation staff are depending on you and planning the daily tasks around the expected schedule for the day. When you don't work your scheduled hours, you are having a detrimental effect on the work flow of the department, which will be reflected in your semi-annual evaluations. Changes to your schedule should be kept to a minimum, with three or less changes per semester being the acceptable standard.

ATTENDANCE

As with all jobs, attendance is required. Students are expected to call the Access Services Librarian (910-123-4567) or the Circulation Desk (910-123-4567) if they intend to be late or absent. A failure to call in may result in a verbal warning (first offense) and a dismissal (second offense). If you know that you need a specific day or time off, you can also notify the Access Services Librarian in advance to request the time off. There should always be someone available to take your call, so be sure to speak with a staff person, and not just leave a message. When you report for a shift, you will sign in and out on a time sheet. These time sheets will be kept in a notebook by the Access Services Librarian. In the event that the Access Services Librarian is not in, the Circulation Desk supervisor will have your time sheet. Because of the important nature of the many recurring tasks in Access Services, the Library emphasizes dependability, particularly in the areas of attendance and punctuality.

In the case of inclement weather, you will be excused from work if either:

- Classes are cancelled (you will not need to call in) OR
- Conditions are unsafe making it so that you cannot get to campus (you will need to call in)

BREAKS

A student working a 4-hour shift is entitled to a paid 15-minute break on the clock at any time during that shift other than the first and last 15 minutes of the shift.

A student working two 4-hour shifts in a row (8 hours total) is entitled to a paid 15-minute break during each shift other than the first and last 15 minutes of the shifts. The breaks must be taken at separate times. The student is also required to clock out for a 5- to 30-minute unpaid break at a separate time from the paid breaks. No other breaks will be approved. Breaks will not be permitted for smoking or telephone use.

REMEMBER THESE BREAKS CANNOT BE COMBINED.

IMPORTANT: When you decide to take a break, you must sign out on the Break Sign-Out Sheet, which is located in the time-sheet notebook. At this time, you must have the Circulation Desk supervisor on duty initial this sheet with the understanding that you will return within the 15-minute break rule time. They must also initial the sheet when you return.

PAYROLL

To avoid any problems with payroll, all time sheets are to be filled out properly. You must sign your timecard in ink or you will not receive your paycheck. In order to be sure your time sheet is ready when payroll is processed, it is best to sign them the first of each month. If your time sheet is not signed when it is time to process payroll, your time sheet will be held over until the following month and you will not receive a paycheck until it is signed and the next payroll is processed. Paychecks and direct deposit stubs must be claimed as promptly as possible from the cashier's office in Lumbee Hall.

STAFF LOUNGE

A student assistant wanting to use the staff lounge during a break may do so. Student assistants may store food items in the refrigerator (you should label it with your name), use the microwave, and purchase beverages from the vending machine. Please respect others' food items. The student lounge is not to be visited while on the clock. Student assistants are permitted to get a beverage, etc., but lounging while on the clock is not permitted.

DRESS CODE

Student assistants are expected to dress in proper casual attire for a business setting. Good personal hygiene is expected. Some individuals are allergic to perfumes and colognes, so please use these sparingly. Shoes are required. It is recommended that they be closed-toed for safety reasons.

Student assistants may NOT wear the following:

1. sunglasses
2. torn clothing
3. see-through or mesh clothing
4. clothing that exposes your midriff or chest
5. clothing that exposes your underwear
6. clothing that displays obscenities
7. flip-flops
8. tank-tops/spaghetti straps/halter tops
9. short shorts
10. bare feet

Note: Student assistants may wear headphones and listen to music while performing stacks maintenance, but proper volume levels must be observed so that patrons are not disturbed. If your music is heard outside of the headphones you will permanently lose the privilege.

INJURIES

Injuries acquired on the job should be reported immediately to the Circulation Desk supervisor. The severity of the injury will determine the course of action required. Minor injuries can be handled using the first aid kit in the circulation office. More serious injuries should be reported and will be handled on an individual basis. All injuries must have a work injury form filled out in order to meet state and federal requirements, even if the injury is minor.

General Policies

No student will be allowed to work when he/she is scheduled for a class. Violation of this rule may result in immediate termination.

Visitors are not encouraged while you are working. Please keep all personal conversations to a minimum of one minute. It is your responsibility to inform your friends of this policy. Persons asking for you by phone or at the Circulation Desk will be told that they may leave a message, which will be attached to your time sheet. Only staff and student workers are permitted behind the desk and in the office spaces.

Computer use during work time is restricted to work-related activities. At these times, e-mail and the Internet may be used for job-related duties. Other use of e-mail, Blackboard, or the Internet should be restricted to employees' personal time. Student assistants are not permitted to use the back office computers.

Telephone calls made from the library are discouraged. Social calls are not permitted. ALSO, please understand that library staff is forbidden from giving out work schedules to the public. This confidentiality protects your privacy. Please respect your fellow workers' privacy, and do not give out any personal information (including work schedules and co-workers' whereabouts) to the public.

Turn off cell phones and pagers upon entering the library. It is never acceptable to use a cell phone or a pager in Sampson-Livermore Library whether you are on or off the clock. You will NOT be permitted to take a break to use your phone while working. Violation of this policy will result in a verbal warning, a written warning, and then termination.

Enter and leave the Library through the security gates at the front door. Student assistants are not to use the back entrance of the library unless retrieving items from the book drop.

Leave your belongings, including your cell phone, behind the Circulation Desk in sorting room 131. Taking your belongings or textbooks with you to shelve your books is not acceptable.

Food and drink are prohibited in the library except in the staff lounge where you can take your break. Smoking is also prohibited in the library.

Studying is permitted if a supervisor deems that all tasks are completed and accurate. Sleeping is, of course, never acceptable while on the clock. Using work time unwisely will be noticed, as your work is frequently checked, and it will be reflected in your evaluations.

Fraternization during work hours with other student assistants will not be tolerated as it is inappropriate workplace behavior and violates the University sexual harassment policy if any physical or verbal conduct of a sexual nature towards another person is unwelcome.

You are expected to work independently, unless a supervisor specifically requires more than one student to complete a task. While we encourage you to make friends with your co-workers, remember that social activities are to take place outside of working hours.

Because all students face the same time crunch and need for materials, student assistants will not have special check-out privileges. Items are due, and fines charged, as with any student.

Use of the staff photocopier or other office equipment or supplies for personal use is not allowed.

While student assistants may be called upon to view portions of videos and other media for damage using fast play, student assistants may not watch videos while on duty.

STRANGE PATRON BEHAVIOR

Many personalities surround us everyday. As public servants we must learn to cope with different attitudes, cultures and customs. However, no public servant should have to deal with a patron's rude or difficult behavior. If a patron should ever approach a student assistant in a confrontational manner, then the student assistant should get the Circulation Desk supervisor immediately. Also, if any type of behavior is observed that seems to be threatening, then that behavior should be reported—as witnessed—to the Circulation Desk supervisor.

INTERACTION WITH PATRONS

When dealing with patrons make sure to provide the type of service that you would expect if you were in their position. Make an effort to help them the best you can and in a friendly manner. Show them where the item is that they are asking for, if you are able to. If you are asked a question that you cannot answer, then refer the patron to the Reference Desk so that they can ask a librarian for assistance. Student assistants should only answer straight directional questions, such as where the bathroom, copier, etc., is located. All other questions should be referred to the Reference Desk. Be sure to speak clearly and slowly when answering questions to avoid misunderstandings and NEVER be rude. If you observe a patron violating library policy, such as using a cell phone, eating, or drinking you may remind them of the policy if you feel comfortable doing so. If you are not, notify the Circulation Desk supervisor who will speak to the patron.

WARNINGS AND DISMISSALS

Student employee dismissal is usually the result of a series of unheeded reprimands for infractions of Library policy. Warnings will be issued for most instances of non-compliance, though the following actions are grounds for immediate dismissal:

- Reporting to work under the influence of alcohol and/or drugs
- Stealing money or property from Sampson-Livermore Library
- Defacing library materials or property
- Manipulating or personally using information contained in library records
- Direct disregard or intentional violation of Library policies

When the first serious infraction of policy occurs, the person will be taken aside, the rules will be explained, and a warning will be stated.

When the second violation of policy occurs, the person will be taken aside, the rules explained, and a written statement will be presented to them. They must sign this statement, which will be added to their personnel file. They will be on probation the remainder of the semester.

When a third violation of policy occurs, the person will be taken aside and told they no longer will be employed by the Library. They will be asked to approve and sign their final time sheet.

GROUNDS FOR DISMISSAL

- Refusal to do assigned tasks
- Repeated unexcused tardiness or absenteeism
- Repeated schedule changes
- Unauthorized use of library materials, facilities, or supplies
- Improper reporting of hours on a time sheet
- Consistently poor job performance or inadequate job skills
- Failure to maintain a positive, service-minded approach toward patrons, staff, or co-workers
- Insubordination

Student Assistant To-Do List

You must notify circulation staff when you are leaving the desk to let them know what you will be working on

- Clear book drops
- Clear staging — re-check in books and re-shelve
- Fill paper trays in copiers and printers
- Do shelf-reading
- Dust and/or clean books, shelves, etc.
- Maintain and keep in order your assigned shelf area — this will include the tasks of shelf reading, straightening books, gathering books from book carts to be counted and other maintenance tasks.
- Take deposits to cashier's office in Lumbee Hall
- Go get change
- Straighten Media section to make neat and in order
- Refresh laptops in closet with freshly charged ones and charge used laptops
- Clean computers at circ desk and laptops with wipes and compressed air

(Cont'd.)

Student Assistant To-Do List *(Continued)*

- Process mail
- Search for overdue and xmissing items
- Make sure all reserves folders have the reserves list at the front of the folder and that all folder items are in alphabetical order — notify circulation staff of any missing lists
- Photocopy and collate materials
- Learn how to operating equipment they don't know how to use — e.g., microfilm or microfiche readers
- Learn about a library resource — e.g., the catalog, journal finder, a database
- Complete a student assistant training assignment (located in Access Services desktop folder)
- Check with all circulation staff to see if there is anything else that needs to be done
- Do a walk-around and look for books left for re-shelving — count these items at the circ desk on the computer
- Do a walk-around and look for food, inappropriate drink containers, people talking on cell phones, and other violations of library policy and notify staff of problems needing resolution
- Read Student Worker manual
- Read Circulation policies and procedures manual
- Read Library policies and procedures manual

IN THE EVENT THAT ALL TASKS ARE FINISHED YOU MAY WORK ON YOUR HOMEWORK. YOU MAY WORK ON YOUR HOMEWORK AS LONG AS IT DOES NOT INTERFERE WITH YOU PAYING ATTENTION TO TRAFFIC AT THE CIRCULATION DESK.

SHELVING INSTRUCTIONS

WHERE TO SHELVE?

1st Floor—Periodicals, Indexes, Reference, Media, Juvenile books, LC books N-Z, Reserves

2nd Floor—Folio books, Government Documents, LC books A-M

HOW TO SHELVE?

Periodicals—return to periodicals service desk; these are magazines and journals with no call number, usually published weekly, monthly, etc.; shelved alphabetically by journal title

Reference/Indexes—return to reference desk; these items have Ref at the beginning of the LC call number

Government Documents—return to documents service desk

Juvenile books—These books are shelved as they would be in a public or school library. This means that the non-fiction items are shelved by their Dewey Decimal number, which ranges from 001-999. They are shelved in numerical order. The fiction items are marked E for easy (used for picture books) or F for fiction followed by the first letter of the author's last name and a numerical designation. They are first shelved alphabetically and then numerically. See circulation staff for training materials before beginning shelving activities. Over-size books are shelved separately as Juvenile Folio in the Juvenile section.

Folio books—These are books that are too large to fit on standard size shelving. They are shelved by Library of Congress (LC) call numbers. They range from A-Z and the call numbers contain both letters and numbers. They are first shelved alphabetically and then numerically. See circulation staff for training materials before beginning shelving activities.

LC books—They are shelved by Library of Congress (LC) call numbers. They range from A-Z and the call numbers contain both letters and numbers. They are first shelved alphabetically and then numerically. See circulation staff for training materials before beginning shelving activities.

Reserve Materials—These items are kept behind the circulation desk and are checked out to patrons on a short-term basis (2 hours, 1 day, or 3 days). They are identified by the reserves sticker on their spine. These may be library books or personal copies of faculty.

CAREFUL USAGE OF BOOK TRUCKS

Be careful when you maneuver book trucks. As you will find, one end of the book truck has wheels that swivel, and the other end does not swivel at all.

Always move book trucks by pushing them in front of you, rather than pulling them behind you. It does not matter if you have the swivel end or the fixed end closest to you, but be forewarned that if you try to move the fixed end of the book truck with too much force in the wrong direction, then the book truck may topple over.

Mind your, as well as others', feet and ankles, or you could hurt yourself (or someone else).

Report book truck accidents to the Circulation Desk supervisor immediately if someone is injured.

HOW TO PROPERLY SHELVE BOOKS

Unless there are new employees who are being trained on shelving, all employees should complete as much shelving as possible before their shift is over. If shelving has been completed, you are expected to complete as much shelf-reading as possible.

1. Check call numbers around the items being shelved to verify correct order of shelf.
2. Items should be upright and shelves should be adjusted to the proper height for the items they house. If one or two items are too tall to stand upright, shelve them on their spines with the call number label facing out.
3. Items with call number labels that cannot be read should be given to the Circulation Desk supervisor.
4. Items should be brought out to the edges of the shelves to make even, neat rows (called blocking).
5. Each shelf should have a bookend at the end of the row.
6. Watch for crowded shelves. If an item will not slide back into its place with a gentle push, the shelf is too full. The proper method to remove an item is to push in the volumes on either side of it, then carefully grasp the center of the spine and remove it (not by pulling from the top of the spine). If you cannot make room, see the Circulation Desk supervisor.
7. Items with damage (mold, mildew, insect, or tears on/to covers, pages, etc.) should be given to the Circulation Desk supervisor. Check for sufficient air space behind the items on the shelves to allow for proper circulation of air. Remove bits of paper, Post-its and paper clips.
8. Any loose papers or library items left at the end of each row or on the floor should be picked up. If the area is kept tidy, the users will tend to leave it that way.
9. Report any problems to, or ask questions of, the Circulation Desk supervisor—DO NOT GUESS!

SHELF-READING INSTRUCTIONS

1. Boot up laptop on shelf-reading cart—laptop should be fully charged

2. Open notepad by clicking on—start—programs—accessories—notepad

3. Scan 3 sections of shelving (averages 650 books)

4. Save the file to a floppy disk with the filename = the call number of the first book scanned

5. Fill out the shelf-reading log on the cart

6. Repeat or

7. Return to circ—plug the laptop in to charge

8. Turn disk into supervisor who will check for shelving errors

LIBRARY OF CONGRESS SYSTEM

Sampson-Livermore Library is classified according to the Library of Congress (LC) system, which uses a combination of letters and numbers to indicate subject and content. Each title in the collection has a unique call number. Materials are shelved in LC call number order.

ALPHABETICAL HEADINGS

Call numbers begin with a letter or combination of letters relating to broad topics. For example, books relating to science begin with the letter Q, and beyond the single letter "Q" heading are more specific topic headings: QB relates to Astronomy, QD to Chemistry, etc. Therefore, when searching for an Astronomy book, the QB series of call numbers will alphabetically fall between the QAs and QCs.

NUMBERS

After the alphabetical heading is a number further narrowing the subject field. The call number for the book, *Secrets of the Night Sky* begins QB63. The QB63s come between the call numbers QB62.7 and the QB64s.

CUTTER NUMBERS

Following the first series of LC heading/number combinations are additional alphanumeric combinations, sometimes more than one. In the case of *Secrets of the Night Sky*, the cutter number begins with a B, which relates to the author of the book, Bob Berman: QB63 .B. The QB63 .Bs are followed by books beginning with QB 63 .D as in Davison and QB63 .J as in Jones.

Secrets of the Night Sky is not the only book on the topic by an author whose last name begins with a B. Books by Samuel Barton and Elijah Burrit also begin with QB63 .B, but are distinguished from Berman's by different cutter numbers. The full call number for Berman's book is QB63 .B473; Barton's is QB63 .B3; and Burrit's is QB63 .B94. Berman's books will be found on the shelf between the other two books because of the following LC classification rule: ***Cutter numbers are decimal numbers, not whole numbers.*** *Often the cutter numbers are preceded by a dot—a reminder that they are decimals.*

QB	QB	QB	QB	QB	QB
62.7	63	63	63	63	64
.C84	.B3	.B473	.B94	.D6	.M6
	(Barton)	(Berman)	(Burrit)	(Davison)	

(Keep in mind that with decimals .3 is the same as .300 and .94 is the same as .940)

TELEPHONE

Telephones in Sampson-Livermore Library are for library business use only. Student assistants are not permitted to make or receive personal calls—local or long distance. If student assistants need to make personal calls, they may do so during breaks at the public phone.

ANSWERING THE PHONE

The only appropriate way to answer the phone is as follows: *"Hello this is Sampson-Livermore Library (your name) speaking. May I help you?"* If the caller requests a specific staff person, transfer the call to the appropriate extension. If the caller needs reference assistance (whether or not they request it) they should be transferred to the Reference Desk. Inform the caller that you are transferring them and give them the extension you are transferring them to, in case of an incomplete transfer. Phone extensions for library staff are posted near the phone at the Circulation Desk.

MISCELLANEOUS

- First impressions are important! Greet all incoming patrons in a professional and courteous manner.
- Remember, the attendant at the Circulation Desk sets the tone for behavior in the library. Loud conversation is contagious.
- Keep the Circulation Desk neat. Patrons will not want to interrupt if you have work spread out. Keep items at the desk minimal.
- Always be courteous! SMILE!)
- When in doubt — ASK!

Access Services Contact Information

Circulation Desk		555-1234	
Reserves		522-1234	
Interlibrary Loan		521-1234	
June Power	Access Services Librarian	555-1234	
Interlibrary Loan		555-1234	
Circulation/Holds		555-1234	
Circulation/Reserves		555-1234	
Circulation/Stacks		555-1234	

EVALUATIONS

Student assistants will be evaluated twice a year to determine possible pay raises, continuation of employment, and opportunities for growth in the work environment. The Access Services Librarian will meet with Access Services staff to complete these evaluations, and will then meet individually with you to discuss your evaluation. You will be provided with a copy of your evaluation.

Students who meet or exceed expectations may continue to work at the Library. Qualities to be evaluated include: quality and quantity of work, job knowledge, initiative, attendance, quality of assistance given to patrons, and contribution to department morale. If your overall job performance is marginal, and if after sufficient warning there is no significant improvement, you will not be rehired for another academic term.

Quizzes, checklists, and other assessment devices may be used to periodically evaluate job performance, and workers are encouraged to practice with self-assessment worksheets. See the Circulation Desk supervisor or Access Services Librarian for more information.

The Library maintains an employment file for each worker, which contains contracts, evaluations, and other pertinent information. They are held for five years for references and verification of employment history.

I have read and understand the library student assistant code of conduct and realize that any violation is grounds for probation, suspension, or termination.

I have been furnished with a copy of the code of conduct to retain.

Name:

Date:

Reproduced with the permission of June Power, MLIS, Access Services/Reference Librarian at University of North Carolina, Pembroke.

INDEX

ABOUT THE
AUTHOR

Kimberly Burke Sweetman is head of the Access Services department for New York University's Division of Libraries, and a training consultant in the area of library management. She graduated with a B.A. from the University of Massachusetts at Amherst, an M.A. from Emory University, and an M.S.L.S. from the Catholic University of America.